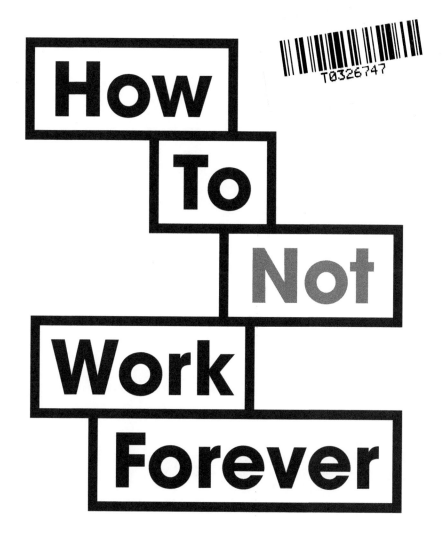

How To Not Work Forever

T0326747

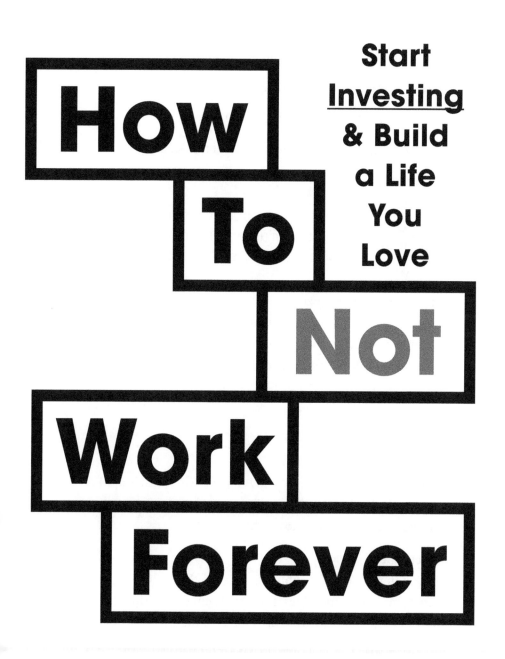

How To Not Work Forever

Start Investing & Build a Life You Love

Natasha Etschmann
& Ana Kresina

WILEY

First published in 2024 by John Wiley & Sons Australia, Ltd

Level 4, 600 Bourke St, Melbourne, Victoria 3000, Australia

Typeset in Utopia Std 10.5pt/16pt

© John Wiley & Sons Australia, Ltd 2024

The moral rights of the authors have been asserted

ISBN: 978-1-394-24886-5

A catalogue record for this book is available from the National Library of Australia

All rights reserved. Except as permitted under the *Australian Copyright Act 1968* (for example, a fair dealing for the purposes of study, research, criticism or review), no part of this book may be reproduced, stored in a retrieval system, communicated or transmitted in any form or by any means without prior written permission. All inquiries should be made to the publisher at the address above.

Cover Design: Alissa Dinallo
Cover and internal background image: © KereAktifGraphicS/ Shutterstock
Author Photo: Arfilmphotography

Disclaimer

The material in this publication is of the nature of general comment only, and does not represent professional advice. It is not intended to provide specific guidance for particular circumstances and it should not be relied on as the basis for any decision to take action or not take action on any matter which it covers. Readers should obtain professional advice where appropriate, before making any such decision. To the maximum extent permitted by law, the authors and publisher disclaim all responsibility and liability to any person, arising directly or indirectly from any person taking or not taking action based on the information in this publication.

General Advice Warning and Disclosures

Natasha Etschmann (Tash), in her capacity as an Authorised Representative (AR No. 1299881) of Guideway Financial Services Pty Ltd ("Guideway"), which operates under Australian Financial Services Licence (AFSL) No. 42067 and Australian Business Number (ABN) 46 156 498 538, provides general advice when discussing financial products, such as bank accounts and exchange-traded funds, throughout this publication.

Ana Kresina (Ana), in her capacity as an Authorised Representative (AR No. 1308509) at Pearler Investments Pty Ltd t/a Pearler ACN 625 120 649 ("Pearler"), who is a Corporate Authorised Representative (CAR No. 1281540) of Sanlam Private Wealth Pty Ltd ACN 136 960 775 (Australian Financial Services Licence No. 337927), provides general advice when discussing financial products, such as bank accounts and exchange-traded funds, throughout this publication.

As authors of this book, Tash and Ana and their licensee principals are the providers of any general financial product advice in this book. The book's publisher, John Wiley & Sons Australia Ltd, is not authorised to provide, and does not provide, any advice and does not endorse or take any responsibility for any advice in this book.

Guideway and Pearler have each had the opportunity to review and approve the content published in this book. Any information here is general in nature and has been prepared without considering your personal goals, financial situation, or needs. Because of this, before acting on the general advice, you should consider its appropriateness, having regard to your unique situation.

It is also important to read and consider Tash's Financial Services Guide, available from https://guideway.com.au/TashInvestsFSG.pdf. Alternatively, you can request a copy by contacting Guideway at 1300 138 138, via email at advice@guideway .com.au, or by mail addressed to Guideway: Level 3, 91 William Street, Melbourne VIC 3000.

It is also important to read and consider Pearler's Financial Services Guide, available from httpɔɪ//pɘɑrlɘr.ɔom/finɑnɔiɑl ɔɘrviɔɘɔ guidɘ. Alternatively, you can request a copy by contacting Pearler at (02) 7908 2290, or via email at help@pearler.com.au.

We strongly recommend that before making any decision to acquire, or to continue to hold, a financial product, you should obtain and review the Product Disclosure

Statement (PDS) and Target Market Determination (TMD) relevant to the product. These documents provide critical information about the product's fees, risks, terms and conditions, and the target market for whom the product is deemed suitable. These documents can be found by contacting the product issuer or by visiting their website.

Furthermore, where any discussion regarding investment returns occurs within this publication, you should be aware that past performance is not a reliable indicator of future performance. When you invest, your capital (the money you invest) is at risk. The PDS will disclose the investment risks specific to the financial product you are considering. If you want to learn more about investment risks, you can do so freely on https://moneysmart.gov.au/.

You should also be aware that Tash has entered into an agreement with (and is paid by) Pearler Investments Pty Ltd ACN 625 120 649 (Pearler) to promote their share trading platform, their brand; Tash is also party to a joint venture in relation to the Get Rich Slow brand, which includes hosting the associated podcast. Some investments discussed in this book may be purchased via share trading platforms, of which Pearler is one. When Tash discusses Pearler, she is discussing her own personal experiences, and not acting as a Guideway Authorised Representative.

We hope this publication helps you on your journey to acquire the knowledge required to navigate financial decisions confidently. If, after reading this book, you find yourself unsure about the best course of action for your financial situation, we strongly encourage seeking the advice of a professional financial adviser. Professional advice can be invaluable in helping you tailor a financial plan to your specific needs and objectives.

For assistance with superannuation, consider that many super funds offer low-cost advice or advice as part of the fees you are already paying. This can be a cost-effective way to get personalised guidance on your superannuation.

If you are experiencing financial hardship, such as struggling to manage debt, the Australian Government provides free financial counselling services. These services can offer support and help get you back on track. More information about the services available can be found on https://moneysmart.gov.au/managing-debt/financial-counselling

Contents

About the authors

Natasha Etschmann
@tashinvests

Natasha Etschmann is one of Australia's most popular personal finance content creators. Tash has an online community of more than a few hundred thousand people. She has a background in occupational therapy, previously working in disability support and as a positive behaviour support practitioner, serving as living proof that you don't have to work in finance to be good with money.

She loves to travel and stay active with lots of bouldering, snowboarding, Pilates and diving.

In late 2022, in response to ASIC's ruling over 'influencers' discussing investing online, Tash became authorised to provide general financial advice and credit advice.

Ana Kresina
@anakresina

Hailing from Canada, Ana Kresina is the author of *Kids Ain't Cheap: How to plan financially for parenthood and your family's future*. She's also a financial educator, financial speaker and parent who works in the financial technology sector, as Head of Product and Community at Pearler.

Ana is co-host of Australia's leading podcast, *Get Rich Slow Club*, and has been featured in the ABC, the *Australian Financial Review*, AusBiz, Channel 9's *Today* show, the *Australian Finance* podcast, the *Girls That Invest* podcast and more.

In her free time, she loves to adventure, spend time with family and play board games. She's travelled to more than 50 countries and now calls Australia home. She can't live without cheese.

Get Rich Slow Club
@getrichslowclub

The *Get Rich Slow Club* is one of the top five business podcasts in Australia, hosted by Tash from @tashinvests and Ana from Pearler.

The *Get Rich Slow Club* began its life as a series of community events. The aim of these events was simple: to normalise conversations about money and investing. It continues to grow with the support of our community.

Introduction

The alternative to working forever

Imagine if money wasn't an issue and you could spend your time doing what you love most. How would your lifestyle change? How would it stay the same? What would you do differently?

For many people, being able to create a life that includes the freedom to choose how to spend their time is the ultimate goal.

Unfortunately, we are told that a 9–5 job is the only path to success (or means to survival) and the thought of quitting your job seems impossible. But it's not.

You want to invest.

You want to get ahead.

You've realised you don't want to work forever.

But in a world filled with Buy Now, Pay Later; inflation; decreasing purchasing power; and housing prices forever on the rise, it can seem impossible.

In this book, we will teach you how to build wealth by increasing your income, investing to make money passively and build the lifestyle that you want.

Now, this isn't a get-rich-quick scheme, as it takes time and effort to work towards a work-optional lifestyle, but ultimately the goal is to create a life where you don't have to work forever in a job you hate.

It's not about doing nothing (because that would be pretty boring). It's about working towards a life filled with freedom and choice to do the things that you love and that add value. Plus, if you're doing what you love and are also getting paid for it, it's not considered work, right? At least that's what we think!

What does having a more meaningful life mean?

For each person, building a meaningful life will look a little different. For some, it's travelling the world. For others, it's spending time with their family. Someone else may want to explore their passion.

Ultimately, it comes down to having the freedom and opportunity to choose what to focus your time on. Isn't that what we all want?

When we have to work, we have to abide by the constraints of our job — in other words, *when* we work, *how much* we work and *what* we work on. For those who are passionate about their jobs, that's great. But for those who want to enjoy their passion and be able to pick and choose how to spend their time, there is an alternative. Even if you're passionate about your job, would you work fulltime if you didn't have to? Or would you switch to part-time work to enjoy more time with family, travelling, working out more or doing something else you're passionate about?

With the advent of COVID-19, so many of us realised that we want a more balanced life: the ability to work from home, have more free time and reduce unnecessary commuting.

By having a better balance, we can also prioritise our health and our loved ones. It's a win–win.

But how do we get there?

Financial freedom

One of the best ways to build a life you love is to ensure you have the financial security to do so. That way, you don't have to depend on a pay cheque. This is often referred to as 'financial freedom': providing yourself with the freedom of choice.

Financial freedom is achieved through creating passive income — that is, income that you don't have to trade your time for. Investing is one of the most passive ways to make money in that your money makes money, and you don't have to do much in return. When you invest, you become a shareholder of a company. As that company grows in value, you are able to receive some income in the form of dividends and/or through the increase in value of your shares. We will get into the logistics of investing later, but the main point to note is that investing is the key to financial freedom — and it's easier to get started than you might think.

But to invest, you first need to have at least *some* money. The two ways to get your hands on money are to decrease your expenses and/or to increase your income. The quicker you get hold of some extra money, the quicker you can invest, the more time you have for your investments to grow and the quicker you can fund your life and live a life you love.

Future-proof your life

When it comes to investing, you need to consider risk. And not only the risk of investing but also the huge risk to your financial security if you don't invest. In fact, if you keep money under your mattress or in an interest-free transaction account at your bank, it loses value over time due to inflation. That's why it's important to future-proof your life and try to make your money grow so that you have future opportunities and financial security.

Of course, we all want to live our life now. We want to enjoy life, experience adventures, and buy the things that align with our values and with what we feel we deserve. However, we also don't want to make it harder for our future selves. By creating financial security for your future self, you may be able to walk away from situations that aren't ideal for you—a stressful job, an abusive relationship—or pivot to a new career or lifestyle, all because your past self has invested in your future self.

What's more, you don't have to pick one or the other. You can enjoy life now, while still planning for your future. There may be some sacrifices in the short term, but we aren't going to tell you to completely cut back on all of your fun spending and live like a hermit (unless you want to!).

The great thing about investing is that it gives you income regardless of whether you're working or not. It provides you with an alternative source of money without you having to put effort into it (minus the initial money you invest — often referred to as 'capital'). The goal with long-term investing isn't to strike it rich with some quick trading. Instead, it can be to get an average return on the stock market, to beat inflation or just to keep up with inflation so that your money doesn't lose value the way it does when it's in the bank. If you're in Australia, this is what's happening with the money in your super fund: how much it grows each year depends on the investments you choose and how the market performs.

Plus, having additional sources of income allows you to reduce your risk in case something were to happen with your main source of income. At least you'd have some money coming in! In fact, most multi-millionaires have at least seven sources of income. How many do you have or wish to have?

All of this provides freedom and choices in the shorter term, if needed. While your goal might be something like having $1 000 000 by age 55, this doesn't mean you can't access money along the way if your plans and goals change.

The sweet spot

Mark Twain is quoted as saying, 'Find a job you enjoy doing, and you will never have to work a day in your life'. That's the dream, isn't it? To get paid to do the things you love.

Similarly, the Japanese concept of *Ikigai* is one that focuses on 'your reason for being' and how you can merge what you love, what you are good at, what the world needs and what you can get paid for. It's kind of the sweet spot in life.

It feeds into the idea that if you can find that sweet spot, your life will feel fulfilled (see figure A).

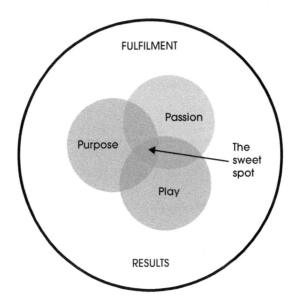

Figure A: the sweet spot in life

So how do you find that sweet spot? Some people are able to easily and quickly recognise it. Others may need to have some financial security behind them to enable them to take risks, which is why investing and building wealth are a large part of living a passionate life.

Financial independence (FI)

The financial independence (FI) movement focuses on living frugally while investing aggressively in order to buy more time and be able to retire early. The idea is that if you invest early and regularly, your money will compound and grow over time, providing you with passive income. That way, you can forgo working and have an alternative income stream — effectively retiring early (if that's your thing). If time is money, then having more money means you have the freedom to choose how to spend your time because you don't have to worry about making money.

What the financial independence (FI) movement did for us

Tash: When I first heard about the FI movement, I thought it was a great idea. I was counting and saving every dollar I could, while working 50-hour weeks and trying to finish my occupational therapy degree at university. Having enough money to never have to work again sounded like a dream. Now that I've had the opportunity to have time off and am fully self-employed, I've realised that I really value meaningful work, and that I like 'working'. I just don't like work that takes over my life and takes away all of my freedom. I now focus on investing consistently, growing my income and spending on things that are in line with my values and bring me joy.

Ana: My number-one priority in my 20s was to travel. I would save up as much money as I could, and then spend it travelling and adventuring around the world. What I realised was that I had a great savings ethic: I was able to set a goal and achieve it financially. However, I didn't know what to do after I had saved my money — I didn't know that I could grow my wealth through investing. When I came across the concept of investing and FI, I realised that my frugal habits enabled me to keep costs low and invest any savings I had. I then focused on increasing my income so that I could invest even more money. The goal for me was to create financial security for myself so that I could spend time with my young family, take a career break if needed and work on the things I feel passionate about. Investing essentially helps me create the life I want for myself.

Why time is more valuable than money

Time is finite. You only have a short time on this earth to live, work and enjoy. Once it's gone, you can never get it back. Money, on the other hand, is infinite in that you can always earn more, spend more and have access to more. There's no limit.

The other thing to consider is that the value of money also changes over time. Depending on what you do with your money, it can diminish or grow in time, depending on factors such as inflation, interest rates and potential investment returns.

This is especially true when it comes to compound interest, which essentially means the longer your money is invested, the longer it has to compound and grow exponentially over time.

Another way to think of it is, if your money needs time to grow, it is beneficial to invest it as early as possible. As it provides you with more money, it also buys you time: you can literally spend time doing what you want, while your money is making more money.

We will dive deeper into how compound interest works shortly.

Creating a life of happiness and spontaneity

Happiness often comes from the more spontaneous moments: spending time with loved ones, embracing the freedom to make your own choices and exploring the world around you. Financial stability plays a key role in this, offering the security and flexibility to take risks and seize opportunities. It enables you to be adventurous, pursue new experiences and create a life filled with joy. It's not just about having money, it's about what money enables you to do.

Building a life around your values

A fulfilling life encompasses pursuing your passions and living in line with your values. The first step to this is understanding your *why* — that is, the driving force behind everything you do. It's about creating mental space and freedom, and moving from surviving to thriving. It could be following a passion, making an impact in your community or simply enjoying the things that bring you joy. Your financial choices will support these things.

How to use this book

This book is your step-by-step guide to learning how to invest for the long term.

Although we would prefer for you to read it in order we know that for some readers, it will be far more beneficial to jump around the chapters and use the parts that are necessary to them during their investing journey.

Part I is your guide to getting set up and ready to invest. You will figure out your 'why', find money to invest by increasing your income and decreasing your expenses, be walked through the important steps to consider before investing, and then learn all about investing jargon and the basics of investing.

In part II we dive into the practical side of investing in order to generate passive income and build a life you love. You'll learn how to build an investing strategy, figure out your goals and pick a suitable investment platform. You'll also learn about investing in super and some common investing mistakes to avoid on your journey.

By the end of this book, you will have the tools to invest, make passive income and build the life love.

***

To keep the money conversation going, subscribe to the *Get Rich Slow Club* podcast, join our Facebook group and find us on Instagram: @getrichslowclub, @tashinvests and @anakresina.

Part I

Get confident with money

Chapter 1

Get clear on why you're investing

The idea of working tirelessly might have appealed to our parents and grandparents, who often link self-worth with work ethic. However, for many of us, the goal is different. We want options and the freedom to spend our time on the things we love and value.

One of the most effective ways to achieve this is through passive investing. Passive investing is like planting a tree and letting it grow over time. It's the concept of slowly accumulating wealth over an extended period of time, with minimal effort, by investing in assets, such as shares, that generate an income.

Investing is something you know you should probably do. We all know we should eat healthily, exercise and plan for the future, but knowing that you *should* do these things isn't always enough.

Buying this book is an excellent first step on your investing journey.

The next essential step is to understand your personal motivation for investing. Figuring out your 'why' is crucial to keeping you motivated, and it will also inform what you invest in. Goals can vary significantly from saving for that Europe trip next year to investing to be financially independent in 20+ years.

If you're in Australia you may already be investing, without realising it, through your super fund. If you have super, you're an investor.

Your super fund is typically invested into a diversified portfolio of cash, shares, bonds and possibly even property. Many view their super fund as a cash savings account for retirement, but in reality your money is likely invested into shares to grow future wealth. Super is such an important topic in investing that we've devoted a whole chapter of the book to it.

Why we invest

 Ana: One of the main reasons I invest is to have security and peace of mind in case something happens to me and I can't work. When I was younger I was in a bad car accident that made me realise I needed to have a plan in place for financial security. That then led me down the path of investing for my future.

Now I invest in order to have financial freedom. Freedom to spend time with my family, freedom to choose when to work, freedom to travel and take on passion projects. Also, my 'why' for investing has changed over the years as my financial goals have changed. Previously it was to reach financial independence (or 'FI') as quickly as possible (we cover FI in detail in chapter 9), but now it's to ensure my family has the security it needs, and to enable us to live comfortably even when we take new risks or make career decisions. But mainly, my 'why' is about having options and freedom.

 Tash: I was really lucky as I grew up in a family that openly spoke about money, so I knew investing was something that I should be doing. I was also really interested in working in health care and knew there was a limit to how much I could earn through my job alone, so being able to buy myself a pay rise was a really exciting idea.

This is possible by investing money into an income-producing asset such as shares, and then supplementing my 9–5 income with income from investments. For example, if I am earning $5000 a year from investments, plus $80 000 a year at my job, this means my total income for the year is $85 000. So, I've essentially used my money to buy myself a pay rise.

Freedom is also a big reason for me. Learning about personal finance from a young age has given me a lot more freedom to choose the things I want to do, rather than doing the things I have to. For example, when I started feeling burnt out from working in health care during the pandemic, I was able to quit to go and work a fun job in the snow while my investments continued to grow. I didn't plan on selling any of my shares, but I knew that they were there if I needed them.

Common reasons for investing

See if any of these common reasons for investing resonate with you (or add your own):

- for freedom: to quit a toxic job or leave an unhappy relationship

- to travel: to explore new cultures or just enjoy some more leisure time

- to spend time with family: being there for your children's milestones, caring for ageing parents, or visiting family interstate or overseas.

- to buy a home

- to buy yourself a pay rise by increasing your income through dividends

- to retire early, or be work optional.

Taking a moment to think about your 'why' is a great way to keep you on track and focused for the long term, since investing is a get-rich-slow strategy. Embracing this approach to investing allows you to build wealth steadily and sustainably, minimising the risks that often come with quick, speculative investments. Getting rich slowly isn't just a safer route to financial success, it's also an opportunity to align your wealth-building journey with your personal values and long-term goals.

The magic of compound interest

Compound interest is often referred to as the 8th wonder of the world. It's the mathematical concept that illustrates how your money can make money, which can create a very powerful snowball effect.

To understand how compound interest works, imagine you have a sum of money. Over time, this initial investment earns money, possibly through dividends (a share of a company's profits paid to shareholders) and capital growth (an increase in value of your investment). The magic happens when the earnings on your investments, both dividends and capital growth, begin to earn interest themselves. Earning interest on both your original investment and on the interest it's already made is what we refer to as compound interest: your money making more money.

> *Similarly to when your money compounds in a savings account, compound interest is when your money earns interest on itself, and then that money earns interest. In investing, this happens in several ways, including through dividends and capital growth.*

You may be more familiar with simple interest. Simple interest is calculated only on the original amount invested, without taking into account any of the interest earned over time. Compound interest differs in that it is calculated on the initial investment plus any interest earned. This is the crucial difference that allows your investments to grow exponentially faster than they would with simple interest.

One of our favourite examples of compound interest is this: if you invest $100 per week, you could be a millionaire in 40 years.

Here's how.

If you just saved *$100 per week in an account earning no interest for 40 years, you would end up with $208 000.*

If you invested *that $100 per week into an investment returning an average of 7 per cent each year, you would end up with $1 038 103 after 40 years. That's $830 103 more just from investing rather than saving. You can see the magic happen in figure 1.1.*

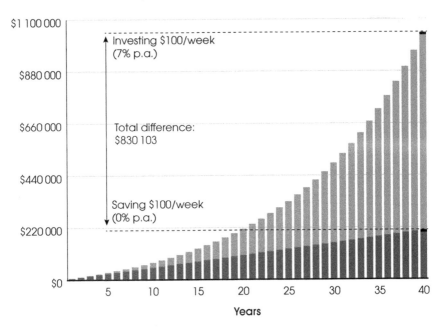

Figure 1.1: an example of the power of compound interest

This is just one example of the incredible power of compound interest. Of course, you'll invest more or less than this, depending on where you are in your life and on your personal circumstances. There will likely be other factors to consider too, such as interest rates on your savings and offset accounts if you have a mortgage.

The important thing to note when it comes to compound interest is that it needs time to work its magic. The more time you have, the more time your money has to compound. Therefore, starting early and investing regularly can really expedite compounding.

Even $5 a day can make a huge difference over the long term. Investing $5 a day with an average annual return of 7 per cent would result in a total of $364334 over 40 years, as illustrated in figure 1.2.

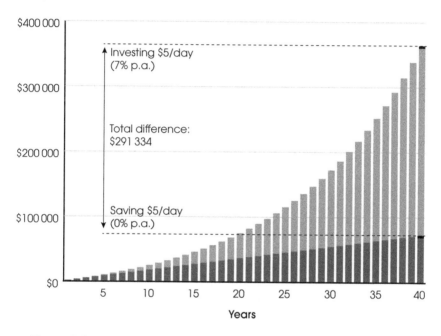

Figure 1.2: you can invest as little as $5 a day for a huge return over time

The main point to remember is that compound interest is your money making more money — and the secret ingredient is time.

The earlier you start investing, the better. But it's also important to remember that everyone's situation is unique and we can't go back in time. There's a famous saying: 'the best time to plant a tree was 100 years ago; the second best time is now'. It's the same with investing. Although we all wish we had started investing the moment we were born, it doesn't matter if you start in your 30s, 40s or 50s — you still have time to watch your money compound.

Let's look at three different scenarios to demonstrate the power of investing early (assuming an average annual return of 7 per cent).

Edie:

- Invests $5000/year starting at 25

- Total investment at 65 is $998 176

Hayley:

- Invests $5000/year starting at 35

- Total investment at 65 is $472 304

Jiaxin:

- Invests $5000/year starting at 45

- Total investment at 65 is $204 977

By investing early, Edie has $793 199 more at 65 than Jiaxin, despite both starting with $5000.

In order for Hayley and Jiaxin to catch up with Edie, they would have to invest significantly more. Hayley would have to invest $10 567.54 per year from age 35 and Jiaxin would have to invest $24 347.48 per year from age 45.

Figure 1.3 compares these three investors.

Table 1.1 sums up the magic of compound interest.

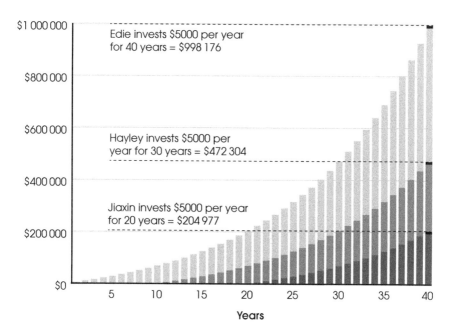

Figure 1.3: time is valuable when it comes to compound interest

Table 1.1: an example of compound interest at 7 per cent each year

Year	Beginning balance	Interest earned	End balance
0	0	0	$1000
1	$1000	$70	$1070
2	$1070	$70.90	$1144.90
3	$1144.90	$80.14	$1225.04
4	$1225.04	$85.75	$1310.79
5	$1219.70	$91.76	$1402.55
20	$3616.53	$253.16	$3869.68
30	$7114.26	$498.00	$7612.26
40	$13994.82	$979.64	$14974.46

You're probably thinking 'okay great, now where do I find this magical 7 per cent investment?'. You'll have to wait until you reach chapter 6 for the answer to that question.

This table shows how each year, interest is earned not just on the original amount ($1000), but also on the interest that was added in previous years. This is the key feature of compound interest — you earn interest on your interest, leading to exponential growth of your investment over time. The longer you invest, the more powerful the compounding becomes. By year 40, your initial $1000 investment has grown to $14 974.46 thanks to the magic of compounding.

The deflating effect of inflation

While investing for your dream house, security or retirement seems reasonable, one pragmatic reason to invest is so your money either keeps pace with inflation at a minimum, or grows more than the rate of inflation.

But first, what is inflation? Inflation is the increase in the price of goods and services, and the fall in the purchasing value of money. You might have heard how someone's grandparents bought a house for $10 000, or how milk used to cost 50 cents, and now that same house is worth $1 000 000+ and milk will set you back $3.20+. That's the work of inflation. If you keep money in a jar, under your mattress or in an account earning no interest, over time you'll be able to buy less with it than before. It's like your money shrinks.

The Reserve Bank of Australia (RBA) aims to keep inflation at between 2 and 3 per cent per annum, but there are periods where it is higher or lower. See figure 1.4 for a snapshot of inflation figures in Australia.

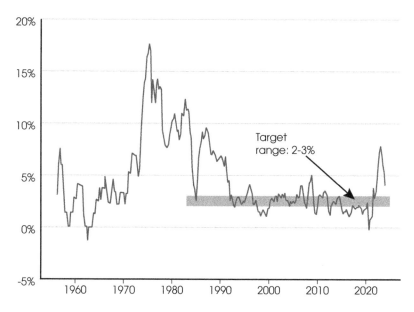

Figure 1.4: Australian inflation rate over time

Source: Adapted from the Inflation Overview by the RBA, made from data from ABS and RBA. © Reserve Bank of Australia, 2001–2024. All rights reserved.

Opportunity cost

Opportunity cost is the FOMO (fear-of-missing-out) of investing. It refers to missing out by deciding to go with one option over another. Not making a decision around investing is also a decision — a decision to delay investing.

For example, you might be tossing up whether to save to travel or to invest instead. If you decide to delay investing for a few years, you are potentially missing out on the opportunity of investment returns in that time, and the compounding effect of that in future years. You can use a compound interest calculator to run the numbers and see what your opportunity cost is if you choose to travel instead (it's not advisable to do it for past choices, as they have been made and you can't go back in time — plus, it's depressing!). That being said, it's okay to prioritise other things first. Life isn't all about money and building wealth — adventuring and living your best life is a balance. But the opportunity cost of that is still an important consideration.

Let's look at three scenarios comparing the power of opportunity cost. All three people have $10 000 and are deciding whether to invest or go on a holiday.

Madison:

- Spends $10 000 on a holiday and doesn't invest

- Future value: $0 (but lots of memories!)

Gintara:

- Doesn't go on a holiday, but instead invests the $10 000, with an average return of 7 per cent per annum

- Future value: $38 697 after 20 years or $149 745 after 40 years

Sasha:

- Spends $5000 on a holiday and invests the remaining $5000, with an average return of 7 per cent per annum

- Future value: $19 348 after 20 years or $74 872 after 40 years

These scenarios are summed up in table 1.2.

Table 1.2: the real cost of not investing

	What they did	After 20 years	After 40 years
Madison	$10000 holiday	$0	$0
Gintara	$10000 invested	$38697	$149745
Sasha	$5000 holiday $5000 invested	$19348	$74872

While investing every spare dollar you have forever isn't the answer (you need to have fun along the way too), investing early is a superpower that can set you up financially for the rest of your life. It's important to find a balance between spending now and taking advantage of compound interest by investing for your future.

Analysis paralysis

So you want to start investing ... what's stopping you? Is it not knowing where to start, the overwhelming abundance of brokers and endless choices, or perhaps thinking you don't have enough money to get investing?

In the world of investing, 'analysis paralysis' refers to a situation where an individual becomes so overwhelmed by the information and choices available that they are unable to make a decision. This state of over-analysing can lead to missed opportunities and hinder your investing journey.

This can occur in all areas of your life. Think about another task in your life that you've procrastinated and become overwhelmed with: starting an assignment, going for a run, doing your taxes or replying to that annoying email. Once we start the task, we often find that it isn't as bad or as hard as we made it out to be in our head. Plus, getting started is just half the battle.

Here are some ways to overcome analysis paralysis.

- *Set clear investment goals.* It's hard to start investing and to figure out your investment plan if you don't know why you're investing or for how long.

- *Simplify your choices.* Instead of trying to compare every broker and every ETF (exchange traded fund — we discuss ETFs in chapter 4), focus on a few and pick one of those. You can always change your mind later. The goal here is just to get started.

- *Consider the opportunity cost.* Does that 0.01 per cent difference in ETF management fees or the 50 cents in brokerage really make a difference if you've spent 12 months searching? Probably not. But waiting an extra year to get started can have a big impact.

- *Educate yourself, but set limits.* With social media and the internet, there are multiple resources available to help you learn about investing. Making educated decisions is important, but too much information can be counterproductive. Pick one book and one podcast to start with, or set time limits on researching and prioritise getting started.

- *Start small.* Investing can be scary, and the only way to truly get comfortable with it is to start investing. Imagine trying to learn to ride a bike and all you do is read about riding bikes, but you never actually get on one. At some point, the only way to learn will be to get on — no-one expects you to be doing the Tour de France on your first day! It's the same with investing: you can start with $5 on a micro-investing app (which is a platform that invests smaller amounts), or by investing $500 in an ETF using a share-trading platform or broker platform, and go from there.

- *Look at diversified options.* Instead of trying to pick the perfect share or the perfect mix of ETFs, have a look at diversified options such as a diversified ETF or a pre-mixed micro-investing option.

- *Accept imperfection.* You don't need a perfect plan to get started, and your plans will change as your life and goals change. Accept that you will make mistakes or won't be able to find the 'perfect' ETF, broker or plan.

- *Consider automating things.* Reduce any friction points that are preventing you from getting started and remove any hurdles that can keep you from being consistent. Treating your investing like a bill and automating it so it happens in the background means it's more likely that you'll be consistent and stick to it over the longer term.

- *Set times to review your investments.* Instead of checking your investments every day or week and feeling overwhelmed, enter dates into your calendar to remind you to review how things are going and whether you want to change anything.

- *Give yourself a deadline.* Set yourself a date by which you will have decided which broker you are going to invest with, or by when you will have picked an ETF.

- *Seek advice.* If you find yourself constantly getting stuck and overwhelmed, it may be worth getting some professional advice.

Analysis paralysis is a common challenge across many areas of our lives, but especially with investing. Choose some or all of the suggestions listed above to overcome it — find what works for you so you're able to get started. Personal finance and investing is a journey, and you'll need to adapt and learn as you go.

As we touched on earlier, we're all investing right now through our super. If the government thinks it's a worthwhile idea to invest, surely it's important for us to build our wealth through investing too?

The challenge, however, is that we're often our own worst enemy, creating roadblocks for investing by telling ourselves things like:

- I'm not ready yet.

- I need more money to get started.

- I don't want to make a mistake.

But these are all just excuses, and often they're due to analysis paralysis.

Investing myths

It's time to debunk some of your concerns by discussing investing myths so you can feel confident to invest.

Myth #1: Investing in the stock market is gambling

At first glance, gambling and investing might seem similar as both involve a degree of risk and the hope of making money. However, the underlying principles between them are quite different. Gambling relies on chance: it's placing a bet on an uncertain outcome, such as predicting a winning sports team, guessing the winning lotto numbers or getting the winning combo on the slot machine. With gambling, money is risked on events with unpredictable outcomes, relying mostly on luck.

On the authority of the Queensland Government website we can tell you that the odds of winning when it comes to gambling are low, as demonstrated in table 1.3.

Table 1.3: the chances of winning by gambling

Powerball	1 in 134 490 400
Keno	1 in 8 911 711
Golden Lotto	1 in 8 145 060
Top prize on poker machine	1 in 7 000 000
Instant scratch	1 in 1 700 000
Horse racing	1 in 1 716

On the other hand, investing in shares is about making informed decisions to invest in companies, typically with the expectation of growth through the increase in value of the share price (capital growth) or by generating income (dividends). Remember, with investing you are actually an owner in a company. You are a shareholder of a real, physical entity that has expenses and generates profits. Businesses will (usually) earn an income or grow in value. It's worth noting that there is a difference between investing in fundamentally sound companies and taking measured risks vs investing in speculative shares, which is more likely to be gambling. Unlike a poker game, which relies on luck, investing in stable companies is not a gamble.

The added benefit of investing is that if you do so long term, you increase the likelihood of your investments returning a profit.

The longer you gamble, the higher the chance of the opposite being true.

So why do people gamble instead of just investing? Gambling often has a lower entry point (e.g. $2 scratchies). Gambling can also cause an addictive adrenaline rush, especially when the potential prizes or rewards are huge. And it doesn't require a lot of research and planning, like investing does. Don't fall into this trap.

Myth #2: It's safer to have money in a bank account

Is money in the bank safer than investing? Well, kind of. What we're really talking about here is risk. Having cash in the bank is low risk, whereas investing can be higher risk. If you have $10 000 in the bank and need to access it in 3 years' time, the likelihood of still having $10 000 is very high.

Conversely, as the market fluctuates from year to year, in 3 years' time there's no guarantee that you will have exactly $10 000 in your account if you invest this money. You might have more (win), but you also might have less. Keep in mind that you haven't really lost money unless you choose to sell during a downturn, since fluctuations are a normal part of investing. You need to be in it for the long run.

So, why would you invest instead of leaving your money in your bank account where it almost seems like a sure thing?

We've seen how inflation eats away at the purchasing power of your money. For example, at a 3-per cent annual inflation rate, in 3 years $10 000 would only be worth $9151.42. This highlights how keeping cash leads to a loss in its real value due to the steadily rising annual cost of living.

While investing carries a higher risk than holding cash, it has historically had higher returns over the long term. This makes investing in shares a worthwhile strategy to use for overcoming the effects of inflation.

Investing also offers the potential for greater purchasing power in the future. There are some exceptions to this, though, such as saving for shorter term goals or for an emergency fund.

Myth #3: I could lose all my money

The truth is that no-one knows what will happen with the share market from day to day. This uncertainty is why there's an emphasis on long-term investing. Share-market values can change dramatically over short periods of time, even daily or annually. But the likelihood of losing all your money depends on what you invest in and when you pull your money out — also known as 'realising your gains' or 'crystallising'.

Here's an example.

Let's say you buy 10 shares at $2 each — so you have a total investment of $20. The share price suddenly drops to $1. If you find yourself needing $10 urgently, you'll be forced to sell all 10 shares at the reduced price, crystallising — or locking in — those losses. If you wait until the share price increases — possibly back to $2 or more — you would only need to sell a smaller number of shares to get the $10 needed. This highlights the importance of not selling during a downtown and instead waiting for the market to recover.

As we've seen, the market moves up and down constantly (see figure 1.5, overleaf), but it's only when you sell your shares that you've concreted the profit or loss. So if you've invested in a diversified, low-cost index portfolio and you've invested across many companies from many sectors, you've reduced some of your risk).

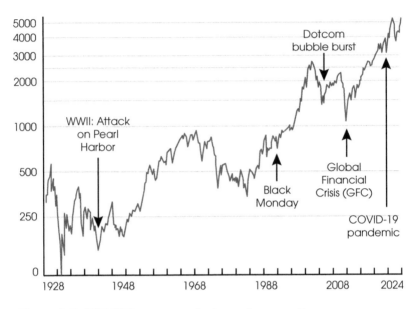

Figure 1.5: S&P 500 average closing price over time

Source: Based on data from S&P 500 Index - 90 Year Historical Chart. Macrotrends LLC. The S&P 500 Index® is a product of S&P Dow Jones Indices LLC. © S&P Dow Jones Indices LLC 2024. S&P®, S&P 500®, US500, The 500 are trademarks of S&P Financial Services LLC. Dow Jones® is a trademark of Dow Jones Trademark Holdings LLC.

The likelihood of losing everything due to the market crashing to zero is low. A situation like that would require a massive global financial crisis (GFC) affecting all businesses and governments. Many will remember the impact of the GFC of 2007–2009, and how it affected people worldwide. But what's rarely noted is that if investors were well diversified (that is, they didn't have all their eggs in one basket) and didn't pull their money out at the bottom of a crash, their money would have grown over the next 10+ years. Nevertheless, past performance isn't an indicator of future returns. The bigger risk can be argued: what if you don't invest and lose out on keeping up with inflation?

Myth #4: Investing is too complicated

We've been taught to believe that investing is complex. It's because there's so much jargon, which can make it intimidating.

The truth is, the main reason investing seems complex or overwhelming is probably because no-one has taken the time to explain it in simple terms that are easy to understand (which is what we're trying to do with this book). 'Investing' is an umbrella term: while day trading, for example, is very complicated and not for the everyday person, investing in low-cost diversified index funds makes investing a far more accessible, simple strategy that anyone can follow. (We will explain what low-cost diversified index funds are in chapter 4 and how you can buy them in chapter 6).

> *Index funds are usually ETFs or managed funds that track an index. This means they follow a predetermined set of rules.*

Basically, if you can buy shoes online, you can buy shares. It's literally that simple to get started.

Of course, there are nuances when it comes to understanding what to buy and what your optimal strategy is — and understanding your risk tolerance and timeline — but overall, getting started isn't hard.

The first step is to get confident with the relevant information, which is what you're doing by reading this book.

Myth #5: You need to be good at maths to invest

Maths and financial literacy go hand in hand and result in some of the best financial outcomes. However, being good at maths isn't essential. So much of investing is about behaviour and psychology.

You can liken it to being fit. Do you need to be strong to be fit? It helps, but being fit is more about focusing on eating well and exercising consistently. The longer you stay on the path of having a healthy diet and moving your body, the more likely you are to continue to have a positive journey of wellness.

Similarly, investing is about focusing on having a positive money mindset and ensuring you are consistent and intentional.

Putting away $100 a month doesn't require much maths, but what it does require is action. Taking action and signing up to a broker, depositing that first $100 and doing it continually over a long period of time is all about behaviour. If you can do that consistently, you're off to a great start.

Myth #6: Timing the market is the best strategy—just buy low and sell high

It makes sense: buy low and sell high and you'll be rich. However, in practice it's really hard to do. It would mean you'd need to watch the market very closely and be ready to buy and sell at any time. Do you have time to watch the market all day, every day? Unless you're a stock broker, this may not be the ideal role for you.

Not only that, but even fund managers can't be consistent when it comes to predicting what the markets will do because no-one can see into the future.

Consider this example.

If you invested $1000 into the Vanguard Australian Shares Index Fund in January 2000 and consistently added $100 a month, by January 2020 your investments would have grown to $66 300, and by March 2020 they would have dropped to $48 601.

Let's consider some scenarios based on this example.

- *Scenario A:*

  In March 2020 you decide to exit the market and move your shares into cash. You continue depositing $100 each month. Your investment would have increased to $53 000 by March 2023 (assuming a 0.6 per cent cash return).

- *Scenario B:*

  You decide to continue adding $100 a month and don't sell. Your investment is worth $81 144 in March 2023.

By deciding to sell, you'd lose $32 543 of potential financial gain, which is a missed growth of 67 per cent.

Myth #7: You need a lot of money to start investing

You don't need thousands of dollars to start investing. In fact, there are micro-investing options available that enable you to start with as little as $5. It's a great way to dip your toes in and see what investing is all about.

For example, if you invest $20 a month with an average annual return of 7 per cent, in 30 years it would grow to be $22 671, which is way better than not investing at all.

Myth #8: You need a complicated strategy

You can basically invest with one ETF and have a very broad and diversified portfolio. Putting together an investing strategy can be as simple as determining what to invest in and how often.

Myth #9: Real estate is the better investment

It's not actually possible to know what the better investment is. Some people may be better suited to property, while others are better suited to shares. There's complexity and risk involved in both investment types. Property markets vary greatly; it's a lot harder to diversify when investing in property; and there are liquidity risks (meaning it's harder to access cash — you can't just sell one bedroom if you need some money for an emergency). There's also a high entry cost and ongoing maintenance costs and fees that are often forgotten when looking into investment returns.

There are benefits to property, such as being able to leverage your investments (get a loan) more easily than you can with shares, which is a strategy many have used to build wealth. And, of course, shares and property can work together as a long-term investment strategy.

Property or shares?

 Tash: I own a relatively hassle-free investment property. It's a newer apartment that's had very few issues and has a high rental return (thanks to the Perth property market). But something that's not spoken about enough is the time and effort that goes into owning an investment property. Once I've bought shares, I own them, get paid regular dividends and don't need to do any more work. With a property, there are factors such as requests/complaints from tenants, issues with property managers, vacancy and no rental income between tenants to consider.

Shares and property both have their pros and cons, but one isn't overall better than the other. They each serve a different purpose.

 Ana: I originally purchased an apartment that was my principal place of residence (PPOR) in Canada. When I moved to Australia I rented it out, and it was lovely to get rental income, but the ongoing paperwork, maintenance and tenants moving in and out made it very stressful from abroad. On the other hand, my share investments were so much easier to manage.

Over a period of 10 years, my apartment grew a lot in value and I was able to refinance my mortgage, which allowed me to take out money to purchase my current PPOR.

I recently sold that apartment and used the proceeds to offset my mortgage interest through an offset account. The goal is to invest that money eventually.

I can't deny that property investing helped me financially, but at the time I knew very little about investing in shares, and had I known more I may have made different decisions. Investing in property and shares can be a very personal decision and depending on life circumstances one may be more suitable than the other.

It all comes back to getting clear on why you're investing. You need to decide what's right for you, which takes a bit of effort (as you've read in this chapter), but it's well worth the time so you can live your best life and not work forever.

Make a start

Getting clear on why you're investing

- Write down your 'why' for investing.

- Play around with a compound interest calculator to see how much you could end up with.

- Figure out what your first step is and enter it in your calendar. No more putting off starting. Your first step could be to:

    - listen to the first 10 episodes of the *Get Rich Slow Club* podcast

    - open a brokerage account (you'll find examples of these in chapter 6)

    - invest $5 through a micro-investing app.

- Spend 20 minutes reviewing your budget and finding where you can cut back on your spending to allocate money to investing.

- Take some time to identify what your values are. Have a look at the following list of core values and identify any that resonate with you. Go through the list and pick your top five. Write these down and stick them somewhere you can see them every day: on a wall, on the back of your phone or as your desktop screen. Checking in with these when you're making a decision — financial or otherwise — can help ensure your choices are aligned with your values.

Achievement	Enthusiasm	Moderation
Appreciation	Excellence	Orderliness
Assertiveness	Fairness	Patience
Cleanliness	Faith	Peacefulness
Commitment	Flexibility	Persistence
Compassion	Forgiveness	Reliability
Confidence	Friendliness	Respect
Cooperation	Generosity	Responsibility
Courage	Honesty	Self-discipline
Courtesy	Humility	Service
Creativity	Integrity	Tact
Development	Kindness	Tolerance
Efficiency	Loyalty	Unity

Case Study

Jack, 29

1. *Annual income:* $92000

2. *Source of income:*

   On top of the $92000 base rate as an electrician, I am on a 24/7 rotating on-call roster approximately every 1 in 5 weeks. For this week I get an additional $300 for being on call, and approximately $300 for every call-out.

3. *Investing platform:*

   Started with SelfWealth; recently moved to Pearler because I preferred the automated system.

4. *What do you currently invest in?*

   Vanguard's Australian Shares Index ETFs; my current home will become an investment property in the future. I also invest in myself with further study in my industry. Breakdown of assets: 2 per cent in Vanguard Australian Shares Index ETFs (VAS) (slowly going up as I dollar-cost average into it), 30 per cent in cash in an offset account, 68 per cent in home equity.

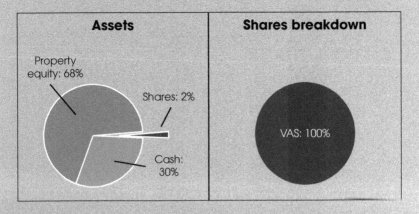

Assets	Shares breakdown
Property equity: 68% Shares: 2% Cash: 30%	VAS: 100%

5. *What's the current breakdown of your shares?*

   100 per cent VAS.

6. *How much do you invest and how often?*

   $192 a week into VAS and around $400 a week as savings into my offset account.

7. *What are your money goals?*

   I'd like to be working part-time in a job I enjoy by the time I'm 50. When I was a teenager up until my early 20s (before I started as an apprentice electrician) I worked for a large supermarket chain. Every day I would go in to work and I was surrounded by colleagues who didn't enjoy their job. At that age, still living at home with very few expenses, I didn't understand why they didn't just leave. As I got older, especially now with a mortgage and other expenses, I understood. Although they didn't enjoy their job, it was secure employment, it provided a steady pay cheque, it was comfortable. The longer I stayed in that job, the more I realised I wanted more in life. I didn't want to go to a job I didn't enjoy just because I needed that pay cheque. I didn't want to feel trapped. Luckily for me, I stumbled into a career I love. But if that situation was to ever change, I would love to have my investments to fall back on. I would love to be able to say, 'You know what? I actually don't need to go to work today/this week/this month'.

   As well as the above, I want more time. I want more time to myself, with my partner and with my (future) family. I grew up with four siblings and a lot of my time growing up, my mum was a single parent. She had no choice but to go to work at night as a bar manager for us to live. As I've matured, I've come to realise I have no idea how she did it. She would work at night, sleep for a couple of hours, drive us to school, nap while we were there, pick us up and then rinse and repeat. She did this, I think, four to five nights a week. She was dealt a rough hand, but she did her best to make us comfortable and she did a great job. However, this isn't the upbringing that I want for my future family. I don't want to have to be getting ready for work when my family gets ready for bed because I need the money. I don't want to have to sacrifice any more time than I need to sacrifice with my family because we can't afford for me to miss a single day at work.

8. *How much debt do you have?* $430k PPOR mortgage.

9. *What has been your biggest financial challenge?*

During the construction of my home there were major delays and I was paying $840 rent and around $1100 in home loan repayments a fortnight for about 6 months on a single income.

10. *How has your investing strategy changed?*

My original plan for my PPOR was to pay it off ASAP. However, I've now decided to stick to my offset account and minimum repayments so that I have more tax-deductible debt when it's an income-producing asset.

11. *What's your biggest money mistake?*

Probably not fixing my home loan at 2–3 per cent in 2022.

12. *Do you have any advice for new investors?*

- Start by getting your savings in order and make sure you have an emergency fund.
- Take the time to educate yourself on all things investing while your emergency fund is building up.
- Once you're comfortable with your emergency fund, pick an investment platform and just start investing while you continue to educate yourself.
- Don't get stuck with analysis paralysis.
- As your pay increases throughout your career, try and keep your expenses where they are.

Chapter 2

Manage your money

We know you're probably really excited about learning how to invest. But there are a few key steps to be aware of *before* you start that will ensure you're in a good position to begin investing successfully.

The steps are:

- *save for an emergency fund*: having a financial safety net is essential

- *pay off high-interest debt*: this includes Buy Now, Pay Later; credit cards; personal loans; and car loans

- *track your spending or create a budget*: understand and manage your cash flow.

We'll explain why it's important to consider each of these steps as we look at them in detail in this chapter. The main point to note is that the goal of investing is to grow your wealth, not lose money.

If you're on an aeroplane, before take-off you'll hear a safety announcement instructing you to put your own oxygen mask on before assisting others with theirs in the case of an emergency. It's the same with investing and sorting out your finances: you have to put on your own oxygen mask and ensure you're financially safe before moving on to investing. Don't worry if you're not ready to invest just yet — go through these steps first and then come back to investing.

Saving for an emergency fund

One of the most important things you can do financially is to ensure you have an emergency fund stashed away. It's paramount that you have some savings you can access easily if needed because you don't want to be in a situation where you have to rely on a high-interest credit card that you can't pay off. So let's talk about saving for your emergency fund.

What is an emergency fund?

You may have heard of an emergency fund, F**k off fund or rainy day fund. They're all the same thing. They're extra funds kept aside for emergencies such as loss of job, car repairs or if your roof caves in. It's essential to have an emergency fund before starting to invest as it ensures you have back-up money in case anything untoward happens.

Emergency funds are there to help you if — or, more likely, when — something unexpected arises. Like anything to do with personal finance, you need to decide exactly what it's for, but some examples could include:

- unemployment

- illness or injury

- taking extended time off to care for a family member or friend

- car breakdowns

- appliances breaking down (e.g. fridge, washing machine)

- a pet needing surgery

- your dentist informing you that you need a root canal.

The idea here is to have money available to cover any unexpected, necessary expenses so that they don't derail your other financial goals. A last-minute festival ticket or boots going on special are, unfortunately, not an emergency, but you can create separate savings accounts for these spontaneous, fun things too.

As we've seen, investment markets fluctuate, and you don't ever want to be in a situation where you need to sell your investments urgently to get out of an emergency situation. Not only that, but there are tax implications when you sell your investments, so ensuring you have all the information you need before making a decision to invest in the stock market is important.

You only actually lose money investing if you sell your investments when the market is down, so avoiding this is the key to making money through long-term investing.

Research from Princeton in 2013 found that financial stress can lead to poorer decisions. The researchers observed that people experiencing money problems exhibited a drop in cognitive function similar to that of losing an entire night's sleep or a 13-point drop in IQ.

Facing an unexpected situation can cause a lot of stress. Having an emergency fund might allow you to pay for the unexpected cost without additional stress, or to have time off or even just to allow you to make better decisions.

How much do you need?

Personal finance is personal, so unfortunately there isn't one simple number we can give you for how much *you* need in your emergency fund.

Consider these two situations.

Sam:

- uni student

- lives at home with family

- minimal bills.

Charlie:

- family of four: two adults, two children under 5

- single-income household

- extended family lives overseas.

Sam will need a different amount in their emergency fund than Charlie. Sam may be able to rely on their family to help out if something were to go wrong. Charlie, on the other hand, needs to consider their immediate family and expenses along with the possibility that they may have to go overseas in the event of a family emergency.

A general rule of thumb is to have 3–6 months of living expenses saved, but there are a few things to consider that might affect that amount, such as:

- Do you have dependants?

- Do you have a property that may need emergency repairs?

- Is your job secure, and how long would it take you to find a new one?

- Do you have another income that could help you through an emergency?

- Are you going on parental leave / having children?

- Is your family interstate or overseas and do you need to consider travel costs?

- Do you have insurance?

Your emergency fund may look very different from someone else's, even if they are in a similar life situation to you since your goals, risk and lifestyle may be very different.

Nonetheless, ensuring you have an emergency fund is important so you can feel financially safe prior to investing.

How to balance saving and paying off debt

If you have debt (which we will talk about next), you may be wondering how to balance saving for an emergency fund with paying off your high-interest debt. (Of course, you don't want to get further into debt, which is why having an emergency fund is important to help break the cycle of debt.) You could start by saving $500–$1000 to put towards your emergency fund instead of the recommended 3–6 months of living expenses, and then add to this once you've paid off your high-interest debts.

Paying off high-interest debt

Once you've saved up at least some of your emergency fund, you should prioritise paying off any high-interest debt. It's important to do this prior to investing, as consumer debt can be detrimental to building wealth.

What is high-interest debt?

Let's start by defining what 'high interest' actually is. Generally, anything over 7 per cent falls into this definition. This may include debts such as credit cards; personal loans; car loans; and Buy Now, Pay Later payment options. High-interest debt is also often called 'consumer debt'.

Financial Counselling Australia found that the average interest rate for credit cards was 19.94 per cent as of October 2021, but as credit card interest is compounded monthly, the average annual effective interest rate is actually 21.87 per cent. And in 2023, the average interest rate for personal loans was 13.87 per cent according to *Money* magazine's website.

This is considered high in comparison to the average return of the stock market. *Investopedia* stated that the S&P 500 returned an average of 10.26 per cent between 1957 and the end of 2023. (The S&P 500 is a common benchmark used in the investing world).

As we saw in chapter 1, compound interest can be very powerful. This is great when it comes to making money through investing and accelerating wealth building, but it can be damaging when you're paying the interest instead of earning it.

Let's use the average credit card interest rate of 19.94 per cent with a debt of $100 as an example.

After 10 years the interest would be $623.

After 20 years it would have amounted to $5121.

After 30 years it would be $37 625.

After 40 years it would be $272 464.

This is on a $100 debt compounded monthly at 19.94 per cent per annum. But, as most credit card interest is compounded daily, this means the actual amount would be even higher.

Look at figure 2.1 (overleaf) for a graph illustrating this example. Pretty alarming, eh?

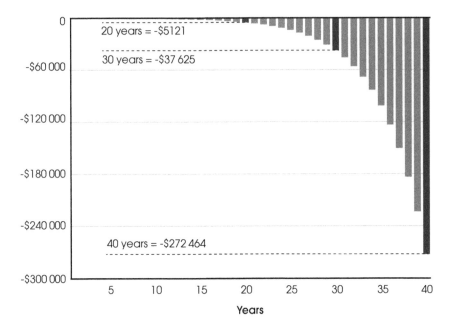

Figure 2.1: a $100 debt compounded monthly at 19.94 per cent per annum

Why you should pay it off

If you're not convinced that paying off your high-interest debt is your best bet when it comes to building wealth, let us share some facts for you to think about.

Paying off your high-interest debt essentially gives you a guaranteed return. This means if you pay off your debt, you'll be saving yourself the amount of interest you would have otherwise had to pay, essentially guaranteeing you'll have saved money instead of paying interest.

Let's say you have a debt of $100 borrowed at 10 per cent interest, and you pay it off before interest is added. You'll have saved yourself $10 (or the 10 per cent that you would have had to pay in interest). This is a guaranteed saving (or return).

In comparison, when you invest money, while you're aiming for a certain return, it isn't guaranteed.

Say you invest $100 in the stock market: you might make 7 per cent in a year, but you might also lose 20 per cent because of the stock market's volatility.

With investment income, you also need to consider the tax you will pay on your earnings, whereas when you pay down debt, you don't have to pay tax on the amount that you save. This tax saving should be taken into consideration when deciding whether to invest if you have debt.

For example, if you pay off a $100 debt attracting 5 per cent interest, you'll 'save' $5. But let's say you put that $100 into a savings account earning 5 per cent interest. Yes, you'll earn $5 in interest, but this amount will be taxed. Tax rates in Australia depend on your total income so the actual amount will vary, but the key fact here is to remember that income is taxed, whereas savings from paying off debt is not. See figure 2.2.

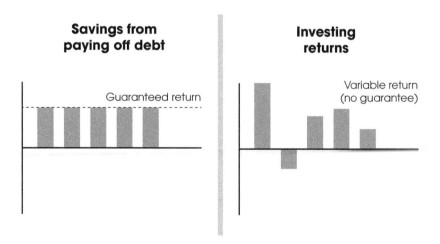

Savings from paying off debt

Guaranteed return

Investing returns

Variable return (no guarantee)

Figure 2.2: savings made by paying off debt vs investing returns

A note on credit cards

Tash: I have a credit card with an annual interest rate of around 21 per cent. I always pay my credit card off within the interest-free period, so I've never had to pay interest. I use my card for the included insurance and frequent flyer rewards points.

If you are looking at doing this too, you need to be aware of the traps. Research shows that owning a credit card increases spending. One study at MIT found that this is because using a credit card causes reward networks in the brain to become sensitised. Yes, tapping your card provides immediate pleasure— but the discomfort of seeing the impact might only come a few weeks later when you get the bill. You need a good cash-flow system in place so that you have the money to pay off the card and not overspend.

I've never had a car loan (big thank you to Mum and Dad for helping me with my first car) or a personal loan.

I bought my property with a 5-year fixed mortgage, meaning my low 2.6 per cent interest rate won't change until the fixed period is up (but I can only make limited extra repayments).

Ana: When I was younger and living in Canada, a bank enticed me to apply for a personal loan for emergencies. At the time, they told me it would be good for my credit rating to have it. I believed them and got a $10 000 loan. I didn't touch it because I always had a savings account and paid my credit card off in full.

When I casually mentioned the loan to my mother, she explained the dangers and temptation of having that money—since it looks like free money—and encouraged me to close the account right away.

Had I been more naïve, I could have easily spent the money without thinking of the repercussions or consequences of needing to pay that money back.

Now the only debt I have is my mortgage, which I pay off in regular weekly instalments—and I still pay my credit card off in full every month.

Buy Now, Pay Later (BNPL)

BNPL is a type of credit where you receive the products up front and then pay off the debt in instalments. This type of debt can be a slippery slope for most people who use it. If you're using BNPL, you're assuming that you'll have the money in the future to make the required repayments. While it may seem like a good idea today, if life throws you a curveball and unexpected expenses pop up, or you have a change in income that prevents you from making those repayments, it can lead to some costly late payment fees.

There are some circumstances where consumer debt is required to pay for essential expenses — but that's *not* what we're referring to here.

Having good money habits is really important if you're thinking of investing, so it's a good idea to get out of the habit of using tools such as BNPL and credit cards if you don't have the money to pay off your debt before any fees kick in.

HECS-HELP debt

You can look at your HECS-HELP debt in a similar way to a mortgage in terms of the maths, but there are a few additional considerations with HECS-HELP.

Here's how HECS-HELP is different from other debt:

- You only have to make compulsory repayments when your income is above $51 550 (at the time of writing).

- HECS-HELP is the only debt that dies with you.

Here's why you might consider paying it off early:

- *The indexation can be high:* In 2023, HECS-HELP debt was indexed at 7.1 per cent, which was higher than the interest rate on most mortgages and savings accounts. Keep in mind that it's indexed with CPI (consumer price index) and can fluctuate depending on the year.

- *Guaranteed savings:* It's a guaranteed way to not pay the CPI increase (which, in a year like 2023 would be a 7.1 per cent return).

- *Ability to borrow more money:* By paying off your debt, you will have a larger borrowing capacity, meaning if, for example, you are considering taking on a loan, you may be able to borrow more money from the bank.

Here's why you might *not* pay it off:

- *Your money is gone:* While you can take money out of your savings account or mortgage redraw — or even sell shares in an emergency — you can't get your HECS-HELP repayments back should you need the cash for an emergency.

- *Potential low-interest rate debt:* If inflation returns to the target range of 2–3 per cent, a HECS-HELP debt effectively becomes a low-interest loan. Should this occur, you might find it financially wiser to save your money in an offset account rather than paying off the loan early, especially if the interest rate on your home loan is higher than this. This strategy can reduce the amount of interest you pay on your home loan, potentially saving you more money in the long run than if you were to pay off your HECS-HELP debt sooner.

- *Other priorities:* If you have higher interest debts such as a credit card or personal loan, it's probably better to pay those off first.

Whether or not to pay off your HECS-HELP debt is a personal decision. It may be worthwhile running the numbers to see what works for you.

Understanding mortgage debt

Not all debts are created equal. Personal loans (also referred to as consumer debt) are often used to purchase items. These items (e.g. a car) may lose value over time and are therefore known as depreciating assets. For example, paying off a personal loan for a holiday to Greece that you enjoyed 3 years ago will not make you any money — in fact, it's likely to cost you. However, taking out a mortgage (a type of loan) to purchase property — an appreciating asset that most often increases in value over time — gives you a much higher chance of growing your wealth, or at least having a roof over your head! This is an important fact to consider when deciding between paying off debt (and the type of debt you have) or investing (and your personal risk tolerance).

> *Depreciating assets lose value over time.*
>
> *Appreciating assets increase in value over time.*

Is it better to pay off your mortgage or invest?

So often, people get hung up on whether they should pay off their mortgage or invest. There are several factors to note when making this decision. We'll discuss a few of them here and you'll find more information on this is chapter 5.

Interest rates and returns

- *High-interest mortgages*: If your mortgage has a 6 per cent interest rate, and the average stock market return is 7.33 per cent (like the S&P 500 returns over the past 20 years), it may be better to pay off your mortgage than put your money into the stock market. Despite potentially higher returns from the market, the guaranteed saving from paying off a high-interest mortgage is significant. Plus, as we've seen, you'll pay tax on your investment earnings.

- *Low-interest mortgages*: With a mortgage interest rate closer to 2 per cent, investing with the hope of a 7 per cent return seems like a more convincing idea. (The lower interest rate on the mortgage increases the likelihood that the return from the stock market will exceed the return from paying off the mortgage.) But again, remember to calculate tax into the equation.

Tax implications

As we've seen, returns from investments are subject to tax, which will reduce your overall investment gain. This must be considered when comparing potential investing returns to the savings from paying off your mortgage. Unfortunately, tax can get a little complicated and the rate varies depending on the income you've earned and how long an asset has been held, so there's no universal rule that works here.

Concentration risk

Diversification is the key. Putting all your money into one share or one property can be risky. There are both pros and cons, and often there are different considerations such as whether the property is your primary property of residence (PPOR) or an investment property (IP).

If you choose to pay down your mortgage, you may have 'concentration risk', meaning your investments are concentrated in one sector (property) in one area (Australia, or even just one suburb) and are not diversified.

However, there's something to be said about financial security and peace of mind when you've paid down your property, which may be more valuable to you than getting the best financial outcomes.

Opportunity cost

As we explained in chapter 1, opportunity cost is the loss of an opportunity when an alternative option is chosen. Therefore, if you choose to pay down your mortgage, you may be losing out on higher returns through investing in shares. However, the peace of mind that comes with paying off your mortgage is pretty amazing too. Weighing up the pros and cons of what your opportunity cost might be, may help you make the best decision.

Making the best decision

Let's compare your options by looking at the pros and cons of each.

- *Paying off your mortgage:*

    - *Pros*: guaranteed return in the form of interest savings, reduced financial stress and a sense of security.

    - *Cons*: potential to miss out on higher returns and overconcentration on one property.

- *Investing in shares:*

    - *Pros*: potential for higher returns, diversification of assets, potential long-term growth and possible tax deductions through debt recycling.

    - *Cons*: market risk, tax implications on returns and the possibility of lower returns than mortgage interest savings.

As we said, there's no single answer when it comes to making financial decisions. That's why personal finance is ... personal.

Other reasons for not paying off debt

We've seen that paying off high-interest debt is not necessarily the right answer for everyone in every situation. Some high-interest loans, such as car loans, can be hard to pay off early or exit without paying huge fees, so make sure you read your contract carefully and understand how the fees work.

There are a few things you might want to consider when deciding if it's worth paying off a debt early:

- *Exit fee.* A fee charged when you pay off your loan and want to close the account.

- *Early repayment fee.* A fee charged when you pay off your loan before a specific time.

- *Tax deduction.* Having debt is beneficial if, for example, you have a car loan in a business's name or you're negatively gearing.

- *Debt recycling.* In Australia, debt recycling is essentially the process of using your income to pay down your home loan, and then redrawing that amount to invest. This strategy converts the non-deductible debt of your home loan (which doesn't generate any tax benefits) into deductible debt tied to investments, allowing you to potentially claim tax deductions on the interest of the redrawn amount used for investing.

Investing while also paying down debt

When it comes to personal finances, you can always run the numbers and have a calculated answer, but there's also an emotional component that's important to consider. For example, when you look at the numbers, it might make sense to completely pay off your $1000-per-month personal loan at 10 per cent interest before investing. But what happens when you finish paying this off? Going from never investing to investing $1000 per month may be a huge and uncomfortable step. Someone who has already been investing smaller amounts while paying off their debt might feel more comfortable and ready to invest the extra $1000 per month.

Instead, you might start investing $5–$10 a week as you pay down higher interest debt so you can build the habit and start learning how you feel about and react to market fluctuations. Investing in shares can be an emotional rollercoaster. Unfortunately, the share prices don't only go up.

Think about some of the times when you've seen news about the stock market. Red arrows and big headlines highlighting losses are common. How do they make you feel? Figure 2.3 is a zoomed-in version of stock-market fluctuations.

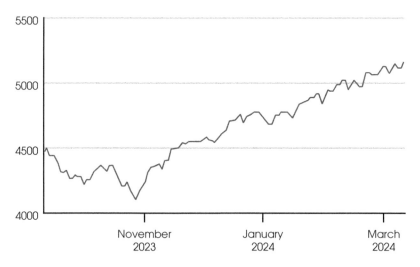

Figure 2.3: the S&P 500 zoomed in
Source: The S&P 500 Index® is a product of S&P Dow Jones Indices LLC.
© S&P Dow Jones Indices LLC 2024. S&P®, S&P 500®, US500, The 500 are trademarks of S&P Financial Services LLC. Dow Jones® is a trademark of Dow Jones Trademark Holdings LLC.

However, when we zoom out (see figure 2.4), it's easier to see that short-term crashes recover in the longer term. But in the short term, this can be quite stressful and it takes time to learn how you feel about and react to these ups and downs.

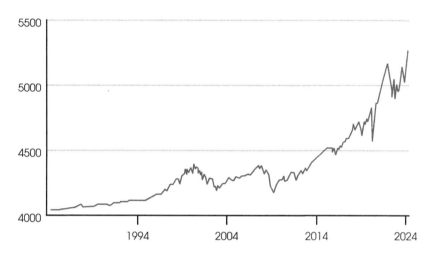

Figure 2.4: the S&P 500 zoomed out

Source: The S&P 500 Index® is a product of S&P Dow Jones Indices LLC. © S&P Dow Jones Indices LLC 2024. S&P®, S&P 500®, US500, The 500 are trademarks of S&P Financial Services LLC. Dow Jones® is a trademark of Dow Jones Trademark Holdings LLC.

The right balance between paying off your debt and investing will be unique to your situation, so do what's most comfortable for you.

Why you should budget

What comes to mind when you hear the terms 'budget' or 'cash flow'? Is it something super restrictive, boring and complicated? Or is it just a plan for your money that enables you to reach your goal?

Think of budgeting as a tool to help you build a life that you love. Once you have a grasp of your budget and spending, you can allocate money towards investing, which will ultimately build wealth and help you work towards your goal (of not working forever). Tracking your spending allows you to:

- create a realistic budget (it's hard to do this if you don't know what life is costing you)

- be in control of your finances and make informed decisions

- allocate money to things that you value and that bring you joy.

How much you can invest really comes down to understanding your cash flow. Having a good cash flow or budgeting system is important because you don't want to over-invest and not have enough money available for expenses. Remember that you only lose money when you sell, and you want to avoid needing to do this at times such as market downturns. It's important that you do not rely on the money you've invested for any short-term goals or emergencies. As a rule of thumb, any money you invest in shares you should be prepared to leave alone for at least 7 years.

Knowing how much you want to invest each week, fortnight or month will also help you decide which investing platform is best for you. They all have different minimums and fees based on investment amounts (more on investing platforms in chapter 6).

You can budget by tracking your spending and knowing where your money goes, or you can create a budget and allocate money for expenses and investing. The goal is to know how much money you have available to put aside for investing.

It's important to be realistic and not restrictive; investing is a long-term game and you don't want to set yourself up for failure. Personal finance is about creating systems and behaviours that you can sustain for a long time, similarly to keeping a healthy fitness routine. If it's too hard and not a part of your weekly schedule, it just won't stick and you'll fall back into bad habits.

How to track your spending

There are many different ways you can track your spending and budget. The secret is to find a way that works for you and your lifestyle, and one that's sustainable. If one method doesn't work for you, trial another!

Here are some popular ways to track your spending:

- Print out your bank statements and highlight wants vs needs in different colours. Does your spending reflect your goals and values?

- Track your spending in a journal for a week, fortnight or month. A month will give you the best overall picture.

- Every time you spend money, jot down how you feel to make yourself more mindful of your spending habits.

- Use Excel or Google Sheets to keep track of every time money comes in/out of your bank account.

Budgeting apps

One of the easier ways to start tracking your spending and getting a good idea of your finances is by using an app.

Popular budgeting apps include:

- PocketSmith

- Frollo

- Canstar

- YNAB (you need a budget).

Budgeting apps can give you a holistic view of where you're spending money and allow you to budget and track all of your expenses.

Splitting expenses

Another way to budget is by allocating a specific percentage of your income to each of your different spending categories. You could start by dividing your income into three categories as follows:

- 50 per cent for needs (bills, housing, car)

- 30 per cent for wants (entertainment, going out, dining out, takeaway, travel)

- 20 per cent for savings, investments and paying off debt.

For those of you who are visual readers, figure 2.5 illustrates this information in pie-chart form.

This is a good method to use when you aren't sure where to start because it's automated and you don't have to think about it too much. The split shown in figure 2.5 won't work for everyone though. Someone on a lower income may need to spend more than 50 per cent on needs, while someone with a higher income might be able to save and invest more than 20 per cent of their income.

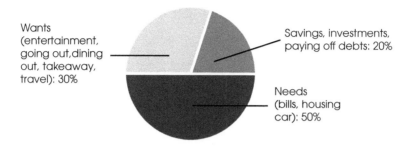

Wants (entertainment, going out, dining out, takeaway, travel): 30%

Savings, investments, paying off debts: 20%

Needs (bills, housing car): 50%

Figure 2.5: budgeting by splitting expenses

Zero-based budgeting

This is something for all of the type-A people out there, who love to be in control of every dollar. Zero-based budgeting involves assigning every dollar a specific purpose or job so you know exactly where each dollar is going.

This is a very detailed way to budget and you will feel right on top of your finances, but it is time consuming, may limit flexibility and can be very overwhelming. It does, however, provide you with control over every dollar and it lets you scrutinise each expense (which can be very insightful if you've never done this type of budgeting before). See table 2.1 for an example of zero-based budgeting.

Table 2.1: zero-based budgeting

INCOME		EXPENSES	
Regular salary	1900	Housing	1200
Side hustle	500	Bills	600
		Food	500
		Emergency fund	100
		Income	2400
		Expenses	−2400
		TOTAL	0

Pay yourself first

This method involves prioritising saving and investments by treating them like bills. You start by automatically setting aside a portion of your income for saving and investing and then allocating the remainder of your funds to expenses.

Paying yourself first is good for knowing exactly how much you are going to save each month, but can be challenging for those who don't have a good grip on their finances yet. For example, if you invested first and then realised you had a few bills coming that you hadn't accounted for, you may need to sell your investments, take money out of savings or use credit to cover these costs, all of which are best avoided.

How we budget

 Tash: When I first started exploring the world of personal finance, I was obsessed. I tracked and saved every dollar that I could. But, as time went on and life got busier, I found that I started valuing my time more than the few extra dollars I might have saved. I have tried using different budgeting apps and budgeting systems, but I found that the more complex and detailed they were, the more overwhelmed I got.

Now I use a more intuitive, 'pay-myself-first' method. I'm always somewhat frugal at heart and find I generally know how much I can spend day-to-day. I automate everything I can, such as my mortgage, credit card repayments and investments. This ensures I essentially pay myself first, and then I can spend anything left over without compromising my goals. Some weeks are generally cheaper than others so I'll have more to save or invest those weeks.

Ana: I've tried it all: using cash, writing my expenses in a book, tracking in an app and so on. Now that I know my regular monthly expenses, I calculate a percentage that I save and invest (this is also referred to as a savings rate) and invest that amount first. My leftover income is then allocated to the rest of my expenses. This is very similar to paying yourself first, except I like to think of it as a percentage amount. That way, if my income increases, the percentage stays the same and reduces any lifestyle creep (i.e. the spending that increases with increased wages).

While on parental leave, we couldn't invest much, so most of our incomings were allocated to expenses and we had very little additional money to save and invest.

That being said, we had a large emergency fund that sat in our mortgage offset account. It had two jobs: reduce our interest payments and act as an emergency fund in case we needed to dip into it while on parental leave.

If you can't manage $100 it will be really hard to manage $1 million. That's why ensuring you have an emergency fund, have your debt under control and know your budget prior to investing is important.

Just imagine if you're living off your dividends in the future and you've chosen a work-optional life. Even then you'll need to be able to manage your money. That's why the knowledge you've gained in this chapter should set you up on your way to building a life you love.

Make a start

Managing your money

- Determine what 3–6 months of living expenses looks like for you and work towards saving this in your emergency fund.

- Make a list of all of your debts and the current interest rate on each of them so you know where you stand financially.

- Pay off your high-interest debt. This will save you the amount of interest you would have had to pay, which is a guaranteed saving/return.

- Take into consideration how much tax you'll pay on your investment earnings when you're deciding whether to pay extra off a debt or whether to invest.

- Trial a few different budgeting and cash-flow systems and find what works for you.

Case Study

Troy, 32

1. *Annual income:* $90k

2. *Source of income:*

   Primary school teacher and part-time freelance photographer. The majority of my pay comes from teaching and I make about $2–3k a year doing photography.

3. *How do you budget?*

   Before 2023 I did not budget. I would get paid and look at my immediate expenses and work my bank account down based on what I knew would come out, like rent and regular bills. Otherwise I would just have all my funds in my account slowly dropping.

   In 2023, I sat down with my partner, who helped walk me through a basic spreadsheet that calculated my expenses.

4. *Why do you invest?*

   I invest because I understand the concept of compounding gains across life. I know the sooner I start setting up an investment portfolio, the faster my wealth will grow for my older years.

5. *What are your money goals?*

   - Pay off my debt

   - Save for a move to Canada (ideally 6–12 months of expenses saved)

   - Put away a rainy-day fund of minimum $5k

6. *How much debt do you have?*

I have two areas of debt: a credit card of $7k last year that is now $2k and a personal loan of $30k at the start of 2022, now sitting at $18k.

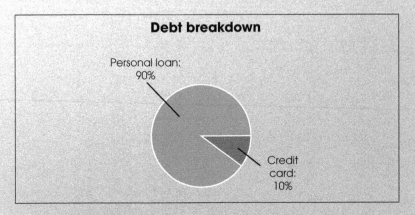

Debt breakdown

Personal loan: 90%

Credit card: 10%

7. *What's your biggest financial challenge?*

My debt. Coming to terms with the reality of my debt has been hard and though I have reduced it significantly I still have so much left to go that it has completely halted my life, as much as I'd like to pretend it's okay. The stress it brings is horrible some weeks. You feel guilty not buying gifts for loved ones, guilty for not having money for cute romantic getaways with your partner and ashamed that your partner has to be a part of your shame. You feel guilty when you spend any money on anything that is not a *need* and you feel poor physically, emotionally, mentally and literally.

8. *What's your current strategy?*

As a photographer, any money I get goes towards paying off debt and I am currently targeting the credit card debt as it is so close to being gone.

I now budget my finances to the $1 and do my best to stick to it, making note of times when unexpected costs arise.

My old way was just paying minimums.

9. *What's your biggest money mistake?*

Not asking for help. After a devastating past relationship ending I needed to get out immediately and during COVID my options seemed to barely exist.

I convinced myself I needed to get a credit card to pay for the cost of moving as I had no savings.

I should have called my parents and asked to move back in.

This choice led to me being in deep debt and living in a place I couldn't afford, leading to two more credit cards and horrible money habits.

Chapter 3

Find the money to invest

Surely the thought of not working forever is appealing to you. Or at least the idea of having financial security to take on new opportunities without financial stress. Otherwise you wouldn't be reading this book.

To build a life you love without financial stress it's essential to get a grasp on how you manage your money. Then, once you do that, it's ideal to have more money to manage. Who doesn't want that? To make this your reality, the trick is to either decrease your expenses or increase your income (or both) and then use the extra funds for investing in order to receive a passive income.

Take a look at figure 3.1 (overleaf). What should you focus on: cutting your expenses or increasing your income?

When we talk about personal finance, there's a lot of emphasis on how to decrease your expenses and manage your budget.

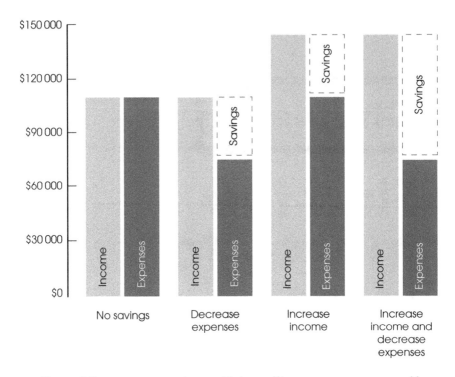

Figure 3.1: you can create wealth by cutting your expenses and/ or increasing your income

If fact, in 2018 NEFE (National Endowment for Financial Education) found that 70 per cent of lotto winners end up bankrupt in just a few years because they don't know how to manage their money. What's more, according to The American Bankruptcy Institute, neighbours of lottery winners are also likely to go bankrupt as they try to keep up with their ritzy neighbours (often referred to as 'keeping up with the Joneses').

Now, the secret to not overextending yourself financially is pretty simple: live below your means and save or invest as much as you can. Spending more than you earn is actually going backwards.

Sure, there's a limit to how much a person can reduce their expenses, since there will always be unavoidable fixed costs such as housing, groceries and transportation. We've got to live, right?

The flip side of saving, being frugal and cutting costs is increasing your income. There's no limit to your ability to make money. In fact, even if you are at the very top of your pay grade, you can still make *more* money — whether that be through a side hustle, selling ebooks, receiving rental income from an investment property or something else. There are always other ways to make extra cash.

So how can you take advantage of these two levers — decreasing expenses and increasing income — to build wealth and start investing?

Let's dive into them separately.

How to decrease your expenses

Once you start taking note of your spending, you may be shocked to discover where your money is going and how knowing this is. Whether you use a budgeting app, journal, spreadsheet, money envelopes or simply a list, knowing how much you spend is crucial in understanding where you stand financially. Having a full understanding of where you are spending your money can help you recognise where you can cut costs and ultimately free up some money.

The most practical thing you can do is study every item on your list and become aware of what you're spending money on, why, and how it makes you feel.

Now, we're not saying cut out every latte (because that would make life miserable). What we are suggesting is to consider what you value in your spending and adjust it accordingly.

The thing is, you can often save money by adjusting your budget and focusing on expenses. The little things are the easiest to cut from the budget (a takeaway coffee each week or the impulsive shop), but the biggest impact you can make is decreasing your big-ticket expenses (such as housing, food and transportation).

Think of it this way: if you're saving money by reducing your expenses, you're giving yourself a pay rise. If you can reduce your expenses by 3 per cent, you have effectively given yourself a 3-per-cent pay rise because that money is no longer going to costs and can be allocated to saving and investing (which ultimately brings in passive income — we'll talk about passive income a bit later in the chapter).

So, let's focus on reducing the cost of those pesky big-ticket items since they're the ones that can save you the most money.

Housing

For most of us, housing takes up the biggest chunk of our expenses — and rightfully so because we all need a roof over our heads!

Plus, with the rising costs of housing and interest rates over the past few years, it's fair to assume that housing now takes up a larger proportion of a household's expenses. On the plus side, *Australian Property Investor* revealed that the median house price among the eight capital cities in Australia increased 103.8 per cent from 2002 to 2022, so if you own a home, you're onto a good thing!

For most people, the cost of housing is a non-negotiable expense. It's a fixed cost and it's at the mercy of interest rates or the landlord's whim. However, you could decrease your housing costs by:

- moving to a cheaper area

- getting roommates or moving in with family

- using Airbnb to lease your home while you're away/ travelling

- signing a lease for a longer period at a lower rate to avoid a rental increase in the short term

- negotiating a lower mortgage interest rate

- finding a job that provides accommodation (these are mostly in rural/remote areas).

Did you know you can call up your bank to ask for a discount on your interest rate, or speak to a mortgage broker to see if they can get you a better deal?

These options may not be for everyone, but every bit you save on your housing expenses can potentially increase your savings. You can also view some of these options as a temporary way to help you reach your goal. And remember, if you move back in with family or decide to get a roommate, it doesn't have to be forever!

Food and groceries

In 2010, the cost of a 2-litre carton of milk was $2.27. By 2023 we were paying around $3.10. This rise in cost is the work of inflation, which is the rate at which the prices of goods and services increase. While food and groceries will become more expensive over time, there are some ways to reduce this necessary expense.

Meal planning can help cut down grocery bills. When you know what you need to buy, you avoid the temptation that comes with shopping. Alternatively, it may be easier to purchase groceries online, where you're able to keep track of the actual dollar amount, ensuring you stay within your budget. Another tip is to sort by 'lowest unit price' when you select items online. When the size of items varies, it can be hard to figure out which one is the best value, but comparing by unit price makes this a lot easier.

Some supermarkets — like Aldi and Costco — can be cheaper than others. Shopping at these outlets can offer a considerable cost saving when it comes to value for money (although local grocers or butchers are sometimes cheaper when it comes to produce and animal products). Buying in bulk often saves you more in the long run, but that's only if you have the room in your budget and home for bulky items — and if you're actually going to consume them.

> *It's easy to get excited by specials and want to buy items in bulk to get the best deal, but it's only actually a good deal if you were going to buy those items anyway.*

Eating out can be a great way to socialise with friends and family, but it can quickly add up and become expensive. The convenience of food delivery when you're tired or lazy and cooking feels like the last option is definitely a time saver, but it can swallow up a large part of a budget.

Here are some hacks to reduce the cost of food:

- Bulk cook a meal and freeze it so that it is available as an alternative to eating out or ordering in.

- Cut meat from your diet and substitute it with plant-based protein.

- Shop at the end of the day when certain items often go on sale at a large mark down.

- Buy marked-down items and freeze them.

- Invite friends over instead of dining out.

- Dine out with intention, so that it feels like a treat and you don't feel guilty about spending money.

- Look out for Groupon deals or the *Entertainment Book* to save money on eating at restaurants.

- When dining out, take advantage of lunch specials instead of going out for dinner.

- Reduce your use of delivery services and take advantage of discounts they send when you haven't ordered in a while.

- Use the prompt function on ChatGPT to help you work out a meal plan that is within your budget and easy to cook. For example:

```
I need [# OF MEALS] [MEAL TYPE, e.g. dinner]
recipes for [# OF PEOPLE] people. Total cost
of the ingredients should be under [$ AMOUNT].
Don't use more than [#] ingredients per recipe.
```

We all need to eat, but we can get creative when it comes to saving money on food.

Transportation

Whether it's travelling for work, to get groceries or to pick up the kids from school, the reality is that it costs money to get around. But there are ways you can reduce the cost of transportation.

- Try to negotiate a lower rate or refinance your car loan.

- Sell your car and buy a cheaper one (that is safe).

- Attempt to only use one car (if you have two).

- Opt for a bike or motorcycle to get around.

- Negotiate working-from-home days to reduce transportation costs.

- Choose public transportation over driving (or, if you can, walk).

- Swap petrol for an electric vehicle when purchasing a new car (and look out for any government incentives or rebates).

- Use apps such as *My 7-Eleven* or *Fuel Map Australia* to find the cheapest petrol in your area.

- Car pool where possible.

- Check the price of different rideshare apps and avoid them during peak times when prices surge.

- If you need to pay for parking, see if you can book ahead (this usually saves a lot at airports).

There are ways to get creative when it comes to reducing transportation costs that can really help your wallet in the long run.

Other savings

Now that we've discussed the biggest life expenses, let's take a look at some of the smaller costs and how you can save on them as well. At the end of the day, every dollar counts. You just want to make sure that you aren't compromising yourself in the process.

- *Lifestyle items:*

  - Be mindful of energy usage. Flick off the switch of appliances you aren't using to cut costs. Unplug and adjust the thermometer on your heating and cooling (you can use energy monitors such as PowerPal to help you track your energy consumption).

  - Use *Energy Made Easy*, the government comparison website, to find a cheaper energy provider or negotiate a better rate with your current provider (doing this annually is a great way to keep on top of any cost increases).

  - Shop around for insurance that has the right coverage and cost for you (being loyal usually costs you more money than shopping around for a better deal).

  - Buy second hand if you need new home appliances or furniture (or check out buy-nothing groups online).

  - Shop at opportunity shops for fashionable vintage clothing to save money.

  - Take on DIY projects that would otherwise cost money — such as teaching yourself to change the oil in your car or how to fix the clogged sink — by YouTubing.

  - Bulk purchase non-perishable items.

  - Invest in your wellbeing so that you avoid unnecessary health costs in the future.

- *Digital items:*

  - Cut back on subscription services (such as Netflix, Prime and Spotify) or rotate them so you only pay for one at a time (how many TV shows can you really watch at once?). And take advantage of the free trial periods on most streaming services.

  - For non-essential purchases, wait at least 24 hours rather than buying straight away.

  - Put a bookmarker on something you want to buy and wait for a sale (such as Black Friday).

  - Use the app *Camel Camel* to compare costs.

  - Use *Honey* and other browser extensions to apply discount codes and coupons to online purchases.

  - When shopping online, use cashback tools such as *Cashrewards*, *Shopback* and *TopCashback* to get some money back. Look out for supersized cashback deals. Sometimes they offer 20 per cent+ back, and you can usually stack this with coupon codes.

Decreasing expenses can have a compounding effect on your finances. Small changes that you make by reducing costs can end up saving you hundreds of dollars in the long run. By reducing discretionary expenses you are freeing up money that can grow in the future, which will ultimately buy you time to spend on the things you love.

Saving $27.40 a day amounts to a huge saving of $10 000 over a year (that's without any interest). It all adds up!

Just remember, you don't want to neglect your life and deprive yourself in the process. Knowing what is important to you and what you value spending money on allows you to enjoy your life while also not spending money on things that don't bring you joy. Finding balance is important, and sometimes that takes time. So don't stress. Making small changes is a step in the right direction.

How to increase your income

Alright! So now you know what to do when it comes to lowering your expenses. But what about increasing your income? Well, this is where things get very exciting because there's effectively no limit to the amount you can make. The sky (and beyond!) is your limit.

So, why is it valuable to increase your income? There are a number of reasons. By increasing your income, you have more money to save and invest. This then provides you with money you can use to generate even more income, such as through investing and purchasing appreciating assets (assets that go up in value over time, for example, property or shares). By having more money, you can create more options and opportunities for yourself.

> *If you're in pursuit of financial freedom, you can create passive income (which we'll get to shortly) by investing any money you earn and increasing your income. This means your money will make money, which will effectively buy back some of your time.*

So, how do you increase your income? There are quite a few ways. Here are some:

- Get a pay rise at your current job.

- Find a higher paid job.

- Start a side hustle or business.

- Invest to create a passive income stream.

Let's inspect each of these options.

Get a pay rise at your current job

One of the main, and arguably most impactful, ways to increase your income is to negotiate a higher salary with your employer. For some, this may be an hourly wage and for others it may be a salaried position. Regardless, striving for a higher salary in your current role reduces the need to search for other jobs or start side hustles, which can take a lot of time or require upfront costs. Consider a pay rise vs how much you'd need to invest to match that pay rise in dividends. Plus, you're already getting paid to do this job, so why not double down on trying to get paid more?

One of the things to remember is that if you aren't getting an annual wage increase, your job is not keeping up with inflation so you're essentially getting a pay cut. This means that your income is worth less than it was the year before, since the cost of goods consistently goes up, and you can afford less than you could previously. Knowing this can be frustrating, but it's possibly a good motivator for you to ask your employer to at least pay you in line with inflation.

So, how do you make more money at your current job?

Apart from working overtime and working shifts with penalty rates, there are other ways to make more money at your current job, such as:

- asking for a pay raise

- advancing your career through education

- talking openly about your wage

- transferring to another role.

Let's break these down.

Asking for a pay rise

Sounds simple, right? The ideal situation would be asking your manager for more money, and them saying yes. The reality is a bit more complicated.

When you consider that the average inflation rate between 1951 and 2023 was 4.89 per cent, you are actually losing money and buying power by not receiving a wage increase (this mostly happens to those who have stayed in the same role for many years).

Before you even have the conversation with your manager about a pay rise, make sure you are on the same page when it comes to expectations. Set goals with your manager so you know what they expect of you and what they want you to achieve. It's not enough to just tick off a to-do list. Ascertain what *results* they are looking for.

For example, if you're in a communications role, it's not enough to say you write press releases, send out emails and update the website. You need to ensure that you are also being impactful in your role—that the results of your work are benefitting the company. So, for example, you would want to show that your press releases resulted in 20 interviews with large publications, increasing your company's exposure to a new audience. You would state that there's been an increase in the percentage of emails opened and in click-through rates, resulting in a more engaged audience and increased sales. As for your website updates, by creating new content, you've increased your SEO (search engine optimisation), meaning that more potential clients will find your company's website, which will ultimately translate into sales (and if you can translate that into profit numbers, that's a bonus!). If you work in a customer-facing role, keep a record of positive feedback or client success stories.

It's not about the work being done, but of the results that your work has created. These key results show that you are a valuable asset and are positively impacting the company. This will show your employer that you are working towards your goals and accomplishing them on a larger scale.

Once you have your list, sit down with your manager and run them through your accomplishments. List all your results and how you've gone over and above what was expected of you.

Now, getting a pay rise is easier said than done, and often there's a lot of pushback from employers when it comes to increasing wages. That's why it's always valuable to do your research: see how much others are earning in the same role and ask what you can do to increase your wage.

Some popular places to research going rates for positions are *LinkedIn* and *Glassdoor*. Although it may feel uncomfortable to have conversations with other colleagues, it may be worth asking what others in a similar role are making.

Another consideration could be to upskill in order to get a pay rise. By taking on new initiatives and upskilling, you are able to prove that you are driven, focused and willing to learn on the job. All of these attributes are positives when asking for a pay rise. Plus, these are great options as you can add them to your resume for the future. However, the downside is doing more work and not being fairly compensated. This is a hard line to balance and only you know what is worth it for you and your career trajectory.

Alternatively, you might consider taking on a new role in the same company. Often, jumping into a new role comes with a wage increase. The cost of hiring an external candidate can be expensive (recruitment, training and providing context is costly); therefore, if you have the skills needed for a different role, it may be a great option. Plus, you can argue that you already have knowledge and understanding of the company, so the company is saving money in the long run by hiring you! (Remember, it's all about how you pitch it to your employer — how they are benefitting from your skills and knowledge!)

If you aren't on a fixed salary, but on an hourly wage, there are a few possibilities for making more money. You can ask for more hours or overtime, which can really add to the dollars in your bank account. Another option is to take on evening, weekend or public holiday shifts for penalty rates. Even if you do this temporarily, it may help you with your savings and getting ahead.

Another option, which is much more indirect, is asking for a more flexible schedule. You could potentially reduce your full-time job by a day, freeing up some time to make *more* money, and spend that day doing a side hustle or consulting. This is not advisable unless you already have a plan or a side business established; otherwise, it may take a while to make the money back that you would otherwise have received as payment from your employer.

Here's the checklist to use when asking for a pay rise:

- ☐ Set goals with your manager (so your expectations are aligned).

- ☐ Document all the key results that are aligned with your goals.

- ☐ Research similar jobs and the salary expectations for your role in preparation for your meeting with your manager.

- ☐ Set a meeting with your manager to walk through your accomplishments.

- ☐ Inquire about other opportunities in the company that may advance your career.

- ☐ If possible, take on extra hours to increase your income.

Our work journeys

Ana: My focus has always been on how to increase my wage through my main job (over side hustles and starting a business). The reason was that I liked the security of a pay cheque and the ability to take stress-free holidays. I also felt as though there was room for me to grow in my role throughout my career.

In a previous role, I took on five different positions with the same employer. Each time, I learned a new skillset, increased my expertise and got a pay rise. In the last role that I held at that firm before moving on, I learned from other colleagues that they were making more money than me, ultimately making me realise I was underpaid for my position. Along with the information from my colleagues and doing research online, I found that I should have been compensated more for my role.

I approached my manager with the research and data of comparable roles, and walked them through all of the key results I'd accomplished in my position. Although it took a while to get approved, I did eventually get a pay rise that was more aligned with comparable roles. Yay!

 Tash: My first jobs after high school were in retail and hospitality. I wanted to get paid more for my time so I did a course to become a swimming teacher. It cost around $500 and took two days, but my hourly rate jumped from $16 to $32.

After that I moved into disability support work, initially at a day program where shifts were typically 9 am to 3 pm. This company didn't allow paid overtime and I wanted to earn more and be able to work longer shifts so I got a job in supported accommodation that was staffed 24/7. I went from working day shifts to working 24- to 56-hour shifts (we were allowed to sleep — this was a type of live-in arrangement — and we were paid for all of our time). This company also allowed paid overtime and needed people to work on public holidays. I made $100 000 that year as a disability support worker. I didn't want to work long hours forever, so I cut back once I had saved enough to buy my first property.

Once I finished my occupational therapy (OT) degree, I started applying for grad roles in OT and positive behaviour support (PBS). This was my first graduate job, but as I already had years of experience in the disability sector as a support worker, I asked for a higher starting salary and flexible part-time hours and was granted both. A common misconception in some health-care roles is that you can't ask for a pay rise — but often, especially in for-profit companies, there is room to negotiate.

Advancing your career through education

Although this falls into the category of your main job, advancing your career through education and upskilling is a great way to increase your income. In many cases, there will be expenses linked to this — such as paying for school or a course — but the impact can be monumental. This is especially true if you are strategic in breaking into a career that is in high demand.

You could also try negotiating with your employer that they fund your education by acknowledging the benefit to them because you will be taking on new skills and insights. Some employers may even offer personal development allowances as well as allowing you to attend conferences for professional development.

Talking openly about your wage

Talking openly about how much you make can be really awkward, especially if there is a discrepancy between your wage and that of the person you're talking to. But the benefits can outweigh the negatives. Pay secrecy contracts are banned in Australia from 7th December 2022. So if your contract was after this date or never included a pay secrecy clause, you can openly talk about pay transparency, meaning your employer cannot penalise you for sharing how much you make with your co-workers. That being said, it can still be extremely frowned upon and uncomfortable to broach the topic with someone.

The benefit of talking openly about what you earn with others is that you will gain insights into how much your colleagues are making and whether you're all compensated fairly. It provides you with information that you can use to negotiate a better salary for yourself. Remember, employers benefit from you not sharing what you earn with others. By keeping employees in the dark, they are able to underpay people without them knowing it. As with anything, knowledge is power.

Getting paid what you're worth

Ana: There's been a few times in my career when I found out I was underpaid in my role. If it weren't for an open conversation with my colleagues, I never would have known. Now, it didn't feel very good knowing I was paid less than others for the same job, but what it did provide me with was a game plan to ask for an increase and hard data to back up my ask.

One of the things I appreciated about one colleague was that she gave me the choice of hearing or not hearing what she was being paid. She said, 'I'm happy to share my wage with you, if you would like'. This allowed me to consider the offer and mentally prepare myself. It never feels good knowing there's a pay discrepancy between you and your colleagues. This can bring up various emotions such as resentment, jealousy or feelings of injustice. Just know that by having these uncomfortable conversations you are empowering yourself with information that you can use to your advantage in the future.

Tash: When I got my first qualified allied health job after graduating, I negotiated flexible part-time hours, and $5000 more for my starting salary than I was initially offered. I found out later that a lot of my colleagues with 2+ years more experience than me were getting $5000 less than I was because they didn't know they could negotiate. At the time, this company was paying $10000–$15000 bonuses to anyone who could refer a successful candidate, and others started using this as part of their negotiations for a pay rise.

Finding a higher paid job

The Australian Institute of Business found that, on average, Australian employees switch jobs every 3 years. There's a good reason to switch jobs too: it usually comes with a pay bump.

The *Zippia* website claims that, on average, the wage increase that comes with switching jobs is 14 per cent, while the average salary growth is much lower at 5 per cent. And for those who stay in their existing role (and don't switch jobs) their salary growth is even lower at 3.1 per cent.

You may have heard the term 'loyalty tax' in relation to consumer items such as insurance or utilities, where a company doesn't offer you a discount if you've been with them for a while, but does offer it to new customers.

This concept works the same way with employers. A 'loyalty tax' in this scenario is that your employer doesn't give you a pay rise because you are already employed with them. However, if they were to hire someone new, chances are they would have to pay them more (to keep up with wage growth) and spend a lot of money on hiring costs.

Therefore, if you're staying with the same employer, you may be the victim of loyalty tax, in which case your income isn't keeping up with inflation. This is why it's advantageous to switch jobs.

It's entirely possible to receive a 10-20 per cent pay bump by switching jobs, stated by *The Financial Review*, depending on the industry and demand. As you read earlier, the average employee jumps jobs every 3 years. However, that statistic changes based on age. For employees over 45, the average job tenure is just over 6 years. Those aged under 25 tend to stay in a role for just over a year and a half. The Australian Institute of Business states that in

1975 the average tenure for under 25s was similar to that of today. Where things get interesting is when you read the statistics for older workers: they used to stay in the same role for 10 years, but that tenure has now dropped to 6.8 years.

With constant changes in our economy, and COVID challenging our relationship with work, it's no wonder people are switching jobs frequently in search of a better role or work–life balance to reduce stagnation and boredom. In addition, more workers are looking for greater flexibility, which the pandemic was able to provide. Although the data shows that older employees are less likely to take job-related risks — opting instead to strive for employment security — job loyalty is no longer expected of employees.

Meanwhile, the younger generations want to feel like they are doing meaningful work, and that they have diverse teams and opportunities to grow. This may be even more valuable than making extra money. Nonetheless, if you're looking for a pay increase, switching roles may be a great opportunity for you.

Is switching roles a good thing?

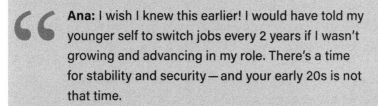
Ana: I wish I knew this earlier! I would have told my younger self to switch jobs every 2 years if I wasn't growing and advancing in my role. There's a time for stability and security — and your early 20s is not that time.

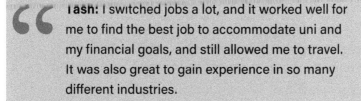
Tash: I switched jobs a lot, and it worked well for me to find the best job to accommodate uni and my financial goals, and still allowed me to travel. It was also great to gain experience in so many different industries.

Consider these helpful hints for when you're applying for a new role:

- Apply for jobs even if you aren't 100 per cent qualified (remember, the job posting is their 'wish list' of the perfect candidate; it's not what they expect every applicant to have).

- Know the salary benchmark of the role you are applying for so that you're prepared to ask for your worth.

- Negotiate, negotiate, negotiate. Be prepared to negotiate all things, including salary, share options and leave entitlements.

- Go out and network and meet other people. This is sometimes the best way to get a new job (*Forbes* experts suggest that 80 per cent of roles are filled via networking and pre-existing relationships).

- Use ChatGPT or AI tools to add the terms used in the job ad to your own resume and CV to mirror what the company is looking for.

Negotiating your wage

It's not enough to find a higher paid job and settle for an increase in income. Often, negotiation needs to take place to land on a suitable salary. Since it can be uncommon for advertised positions to share compensation rates publicly, it's incredibly important to go into a wage negotiation prepared.

Here are some of the steps you need to take to ensure you come out on top when negotiating:

1. *Do your research and know the going rate for the role.*

   Before you get into a negotiation regarding salary, it's important to be prepared and know what your salary expectation is. You may have an idea that you'd like to be paid 5 per cent more than you currently are, and are happy to settle on that salary; however, unless you do research, you won't know what a role is actually worth. The same role may have a sliding scale depending on your experience, and it's valuable to know that up front. Therefore, having an idea of what the position would pay is a data point that may help you in your negotiations.

Tools such as *whatsthesalary.com* let you copy-paste a job posting from *Seek* to find out the salary range. Similarly, websites such as *levels.fyi* and *Glassdoor* are great places to see what the going rate is for roles and seniority at various companies.

Knowing the range for a role can provide you with room to negotiate and also enable you to know your worth.

2. *Never share your wage expectations first.*

Ask the recruiter or interviewer what the salary being offered is prior to telling them your number. The recruiter usually has a range in mind, and it's more beneficial to you to have them share their range first. As they are the ones hiring, they've already budgeted for the role. By knowing their number, you can have an idea of where that sits with your expectations.

If the recruiter does ask you for your salary expectations, you can respond with, 'What do you usually pay someone in this position?' Alternatively, if you are pressed for a number, you can say the following: 'I'd like to learn more about the role to understand its full scope before I set my salary expectation'. This defers the conversation to a later time when you will feel more comfortable talking about salary expectations (which is usually when you have a better idea of the role and the organisation).

Also, if you get asked what you make in your current role, never ever share that information. Instead, say something along the lines of, 'This position is different from my current role, so I would like to understand the responsibilities further to determine an appropriate salary'.

The interviewer may continue to push, in which case you can say something like, 'I'd appreciate it if you could make an offer based on what you budgeted for this position. I'll be happy to consider things from there'.

3. *If you need to state a number, provide a range instead.*

    There may be times where you're cornered into providing a number when it comes to your salary expectation. If this is the case, ensure you've done your research and know your expected rate. Offer a range, with your rate being at the lower end.

    For example, if you're looking to be compensated $70 000 a year, then state something along the lines of, 'The range I've been looking at is between $75 000 and 95 000'. This provides room for negotiation, which may land you at a higher amount such as $80 000.

    Stating a range over an exact number allows for both parties to negotiate and gives wiggle room in terms of expectations. It also anchors the number, meaning the first number mentioned usually has a significant weighting and is the starting point of the negotiation process.

4. *Have a list of non-monetary items you can negotiate on.*

    Although the goal is to increase your income when it comes to salary negotiations, that's not the only thing that drives people to take on a new role. Often, there are non-monetary items you can negotiate to ensure you're supported and have a better working environment.

    Some of the things worth considering are:

    - *Leave entitlement.* Instead of a higher wage, you can request to have more paid leave, ensuring you get more down time. This may also be the time to ask about parental leave policies and long service leave.

    - *A flexible working schedule.* You may want to start earlier one day or later another. Now is the time to negotiate these expectations.

    - *Working from home.* If WFH is important to you, this may be something you want to capture in your contract.

    - *Professional development opportunities.* You may want to take on some learning in the future. Find out how the company can support your goals.

    - *HECS debt repayment.* Some companies may be willing to assist you in paying down your debt.

    - *Share options.* During negotiations, it's possible to ask if you can hold shares in the company.

- *Bonuses.* If your role is a result-focused one, you can ask to receive a bonus if you've reached your expected targets.

- *Equipment*: Your company may be willing to compensate you for any technology or equipment that you may be using to do your job.

List all of the nice-to-have items and see if there is anything that the hiring company may be willing to provide. This can be a great opportunity to receive non-monetary compensation, which can support you in your career growth.

5. *Use a spreadsheet to run various scenarios when it comes to your salary negotiation.*

   For most new roles, compensation is pretty straight-forward: you receive a wage and super, and that's it. But there may be other things you want to consider.

   Is your wage inclusive or exclusive of super? What is the take-home pay after tax? Are there any share options you can consider?

   By running various scenarios in a spreadsheet you can have an idea of your total compensation package.

   As an example, whether your wage is *inclusive* or *exclusive* of super can make a difference to your take-home and overall pay.

   At the time of writing, super is paid at 11 per cent by employers, but that's slated to go up in the next few years.

Now, if your gross salary is $70 000 *inclusive* of super, that means your annual base pay is $63 063 because $6937 will be paid into your super annually by your employer.

However, if your gross salary is $70 000 *exclusive* of super, then your base pay is $70 000. In addition, $7700 will be paid into your super annually by your employer. So your overall compensation is actually $77 700.

That's a difference of $6937 in base pay, and $763 in super each year.

A small change to a contract can make a world of difference to your pay cheque. So it's good to run a few different scenarios and to be informed in case numbers are discussed.

Starting a side hustle or business

Earning money on the side is something that a lot of people pursue. According to an IRS study in 2015, millionaires have up to seven income streams. Surely we can have more than one as well. What's more, having additional income streams reduces your overall financial risk in case you were to lose your primary job.

When it comes to jobs other than your main one, one option is to set up a passive income stream (we promise — we're getting to that). Another is to have a side hustle that supplements your income. Then there's the option of starting your own business and having full control over your work, hours and pay.

Starting a business may sound daunting at first. But even just having a side project that brings in a bit of money—such as making pottery or landscaping on occasion—can be a small step in the right direction when it comes to slipping a few extra dollars into your pocket.

While we can't list all the options of side hustles and businesses, here are a few to consider.

- *Small gigs.* There are a lot of things you can do that fall under the gig economy, such as being an Uber driver, completing odd jobs on Airtasker, walking dogs or pet sitting, setting up a room for Airbnb or even partaking in online surveys for customer research.

- *A monetised hobby.* If you are already passionate about a hobby, there's no harm in seeing if it can bring in money. If you're a photographer or artist, why not sell your crafts and make some money?

- *Unwanted items.* If you've got a lot of things sitting around not being used, you can make some extra money by selling them online on *Marketplace* or *Gumtree*. Or, if upcycling is your thing, you can even sell them for more than you originally bought them for.

- *Freelance or consulting work.* If you're a specialist in a field, you may be able to do additional work alongside your regular job. Even consulting for a new company, or freelance writing for a short period of time, can provide you with invaluable experience and pay.

- *Content creation.* If you are passionate about sharing your views on social media, you may be able to get paid to create content on your own or others' channels. (Tash started @tashinvests as a passion project that evolved over several years.)

- *A business of your own.* If you have a skillset that you can offer as a service or an idea you can monetise, you can start a business on the side. Although this may take a lot of time up front, it can end up being lucrative and could ultimately become your full-time gig.

There are countless other side hustles and business ideas you can pursue. Of course, most of them take up time initially, but it's a good way to see what you like and whether it can evolve into something bigger (provided that's what you want).

Side hustles can grow to be much more

 Tash: Side hustles can be a great way to develop new skills, as well as your personal brand and network. I started off studying occupational therapy and working in health care. I now create financial education content, co-host an investing podcast and do some money coaching on the side. I never would have known this is what I wanted to do without starting a side hobby creating content on Instagram.

Invest to create a passive income stream

Yes, it's time to talk about passive income!

Passive income is the dream. Making money while you do nothing (or very little) sounds great, doesn't it?

There are plenty of options available when it comes to earning a passive income. However, they may take effort and time to set up, along with an upfront cost. Plus, there may be time and effort needed to promote and market a product that produces passive income. On top of that, a lot of passive-income ideas are digital, meaning some level of technical competency may be required — which explains the argument of it not being truly 'passive'. Nonetheless, if the goal is to increase your income, some of these options may be valuable to you.

- *Digital products.* These can be in the form of courses, ebooks, recordings or templates that you create once but can sell multiple times.

- *Affiliate marketing.* If you have high traffic going to your website or social channels, you can make money from your audience clicking through and purchasing products.

- *Writing a book.* The royalties of a book or audio book are paid to you once the book is published.

- *Print-on-demand designs.* Many websites sell artwork that can be printed on demand, meaning you design once, but can sell often without needing to do fulfilment on the products (that is, creating and shipping them out).

- *App or website development.* Although this can also be seen as a business venture, depending on how passive the work is, it may be possible to receive passive income from it.

One trick is to think of the skillset you have and how you could create a product that can be sold over and over again. This may relate to your job or it may just be a passion project. The positive is that this is something you can trial while working in your primary role to find out whether you can make some money on the side.

Earning rental income

Another passive way to earn money is through rental income (if you own an investment property). It's often argued that rental income isn't truly passive since there's a lot of effort and time involved, including administration, dealing with tenants or a property manager, and regular maintenance of the property. In Australia, negative gearing is a strategy used to reduce taxable income. Negative gearing occurs when the costs of owning a rental property—including interest on the loan, repairs and management fees — exceed the income generated from rent. This loss can be deducted from your overall taxable income and may result in lowering your tax bill. However, this relies on a long-term increase on the property's value to eventually make a profit. Investing in property is not always an immediate or guaranteed way to make money.

The idea, however, is that you don't actually have to exchange your time for money the way you do in a regular job, making it much more passive than working 9–5.

With investment properties, the upfront cost can be relatively high. Stamp duty, building and pest inspections, a solicitor/

conveyancer and possibly a buyer's agent are just a few of the large upfront costs. These, along with the deposit (usually around 20 per cent of the property price) and the ongoing mortgage payments can make this a pricey venture.

However, there are a lot of positives, especially if the property is cash-flow positive (which is also referred to as being positively geared). If the rental income is higher than all of the expenses (including mortgage, insurance, strata fees and body-corporate fees) then it can be a great addition to your income.

The other plus side of owning an investment property is that, ideally, the property value will go up over the long term so it can then be sold for a profit. For example, *corelogic.com.au* reported that, on average, houses in Australia have gone up 382 per cent over the past 30 years. In annual compounding terms, this is an average rise of 5.4 per cent per year. And the Real Estate Institute of Australia (REIA) found that rent has also increased, on average, by 39.3 per cent since 2002. So, having a rental property can definitely be an option when it comes to increasing your income. But it's important to remember that past performance is not a reliable indicator of future performance — in other words, the fact that house prices have gone up a lot in the past doesn't mean they will continue to do so.

Investing in shares

Making money while you sleep is pretty sweet, and that's literally how you can make money from investing in shares. In a nutshell, you buy shares, which means you own a part of a company. The company makes a profit, and you are paid back in the form of dividends. As the company grows, the money you invested also grows and compounds over time, making you more money.

Share investing is a bit more complex than that, but it is an incredibly impactful way to make money. We'll give you the full run-down on share investing soon.

The one thing worth noting when it comes to investing in shares is that the reason it's a powerful way of generating income is because it's one of the truest forms of passive income. There is very little management and oversight needed when it comes to shares (provided you invested in a broad, diversified, low-cost index fund). The only challenge with investing is coming up with some cash that you can use to get started. You'll remember from earlier that while you can invest with as little as $5, that won't result in a large amount of passive income. But you can continue to add money: buying more shares results in more dividends and in your money compounding (see figure 3.2).

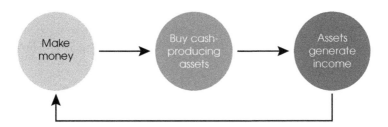

Figure 3.2: how buying cash-producing assets can generate passive income

Ultimately, you want to increase your income in order to buy more income-generating assets — in this case, shares — so that you can receive dividends. You can then use your dividends along with your money to buy even more assets, which will generate even more income. That's how to get wealthy and stay wealthy.

Unfortunately, there's no get-rich-quick solution when it comes to passive income.

Think about the fact that building an audience to sell products to can take years of work without financial reward.

And property comes with many extra expenses and usually 30 years of mortgage payments before you can enjoy the full rental return as passive income.

Meanwhile, if you had $100 000 invested in shares returning an annual dividend of 3 per cent, you'd generate $3000 a year in passive income, before taxes. That's why passive income is the dream — but it also takes time to build.

Mind the gap

Now that you know what steps to take to reduce your expenses and increase your income, let's talk about minding the gap.

No, this isn't the gap at the train station. This is the gap between your income and expenses, arguably the most important factor in growing your wealth.

The more you can reduce your expenses while increasing your income, the larger the money gap available to you for saving and investing. If your expenses are higher than your income, chances are you have debt. If your expenses and income are exactly the same, that means any income coming in goes to expenses, resulting in your living pay cheque to pay cheque — meaning there's really no gap. Figure 3.3 demonstrates this.

By minding the gap between your income and expenses, and ensuring that it's as big as comfortably possible, you will have more money to use for investing (which will generate more money for you).

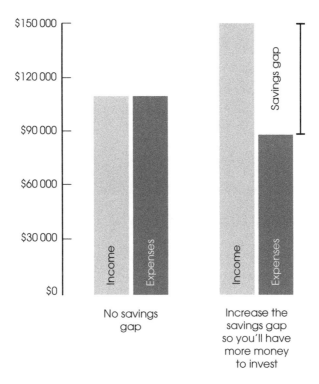

Figure 3.3: the gap is the difference between your income and your expenses

Another way to think about the gap is by focusing on your 'savings rate'. The savings rate is usually calculated as a percentage of what you can save and invest of your overall income. Whether you can only put away a small amount (such as 10 per cent) of your pay cheque or whether you strive for upwards of 50 per cent in savings, by actively tracking your savings rate and increasing it, you'll have more money to invest to help you reach your financial goals more quickly.

By actively reducing your expenses by 5 per cent you are effectively increasing the gap by 5 per cent, and due to having lower expenses, you need less money, or passive income, to cover the cost of your expenses.

Think of your expenses and income as two levers you are able to adjust and flex to maximise the gap. By doing both actively — reducing your expenses *and* increasing your income — you'll create the biggest impact on your finances and investing future, enabling you to not work forever.

Make a start

Finding the money to invest

- Look at your overall expenses and see what items you can eliminate or reduce.

- For your primary job, research online or talk to colleagues to see if you are being compensated fairly.

- If you believe it's time to discuss a pay rise with your employer, start documenting all the ways you've provided value to the company and set a time to talk about your future goals and compensation.

- If you have time, attempt to create another income stream, whether it's active or passive. Set a goal of making some money by pursuing a side hustle.

Case Study

Lauren, 33

1. *Annual income:*

   Me: $70 608; $8944.27 through my own business and side hustles in 2022. My husband: $103 127.

2. *Source of income:*

   I have made more than $16 000 this year through my coaching and road-trip businesses as well as other small side hustles.

3. *How do you budget?*

   We use the bucket method alongside zero-based budgeting. Every dollar we earn is allocated and given a job. Our money is currently split into the following account 'buckets', with the majority being in our mortgage offset:

   - regular bills (fortnightly/monthly direct debits)
   - variable bills (bills that fluctuate; we average these across the year to determine the fortnightly amounts):
     - emergency fund and mortgage repayment
     - everyday expenses (groceries, petrol and takeaway)
     - investing
     - holidays
     - gifts and celebrations
     - my splurge
     - my husband's splurge
     - family splurge.

4. *What do you currently invest in?*

We currently have $20 000+ in investment bonds as a tax-effective way of investing (with the guidance of our financial advisor). We also have approximately $3000 invested in other shares.

5. *What was the reason for seeing a financial advisor?*

Originally, the trigger for seeing a financial advisor was to have some reassurance that we were on the right track with our finances. I didn't want to get 15 years down the track and regret not getting the advice. We also wanted to ensure we were minimising our tax in the most effective way. Since working with a financial advisor, we now feel confident that we have our insurance in order, our investing strategy organised, tax minimised and have someone in our court who isn't emotionally attached to our financial situation like we are.

6. *What's the breakdown of your shares?*

$20 000 is invested in a Vanguard high-growth portfolio investment bond. The breakdown of the $3000 we invested early on is 42 per cent VDHG; 20 per cent Wesfarmers; 38 per cent CLNE (a clean energy ETF).

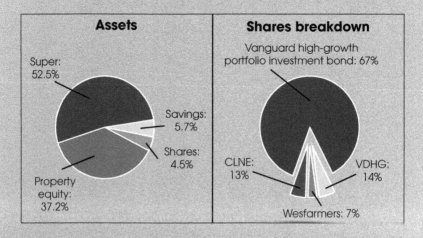

7. *Do you have any assets outside of your shares and home equity?*

   We also have:

   - $188000 in house equity
   - approximately $29000 in savings
   - $265000 in super between us.

8. *How much do you invest and how often?*

   We currently invest $866 every month.

9. *What are your money goals?*

   We are investing to fast-track our way to financial freedom. Financial freedom for us is having the flexibility to be anywhere in the world while working and/or doing something we love when we choose to, not because we have to.

10. *How much debt do you have?*

    Mortgage: $330000 left to pay and an equity loan of $192000, but we have only used $3000 of that equity loan (for education and personal development purposes). Therefore, total debt is $333000.

11. *What's your biggest financial challenge?*

    I feel very fortunate that our biggest challenge at the moment is increasing our income to invest further.

12. *What's your investing strategy?*

    We are investing in investment bonds that are tax effective after 10 years. We dollar-cost average into these investment bonds with $000 a month. [You'll find an explanation for dollar-cost averaging in chapter 5.]

13. *What's your biggest money mistake?*

    Hoarding my money as a saver when I was younger and not looking into investing until my early 30s.

14. *How do you save/invest for your kids?*

Via the investment bonds mentioned above. These are for our kids; however, we may use part of them as a family in the future too.

Chapter 4

Investing
basics

So you've found money to invest with. Congratulations! Next, it's time to learn some investing basics.

Investing is one of the best ways to create passive income so you can replace your income and not have to work forever. But the jargon can be quite overwhelming! For example:

- *bull market*—a market in which share prices are increasing

- *basis points*—the percentage change in value of a financial unit: one basis point is 0.01 per cent and 30 basis points (also known as bips) is 0.30 per cent

- *dividend yield*—the income ratio of a share described as a percentage.

These terms can be mind-boggling when you first hear or read them, but we'll break everything down so you can feel confident talking about financial concepts yourself.

Why does investing come with such complicated jargon? Well, it's possibly because if you don't understand the terminology, then someone who does can charge you a hefty price to help you out. Ignorance isn't always bliss!

Similarly, if you don't have the knowledge to decipher the hieroglyphics and concepts used in finance, then others can take advantage of your lack of financial literacy. (AMP found that 36 per cent of adults in Australia were financially illiterate.)

Fortunately, as with anything, financial literacy and investing can be taught. But if you don't have the right teacher and opportunity, how can you learn? For many of us, it's not something we were taught as children (unless we were very lucky and privileged).

Investing can be compared to going to the gym: you know it's good for you and that you should do it, but it's totally intimidating, especially if you don't know how to use the free weights or the squat racks. Until someone walks you through the whole process, you won't feel confident enough to smash through your deadlifts knowing your form is right.

So, let's start our investing journey now by running through what investing actually is.

Investing 101

What is investing? Let's break it down.

The definition of 'invest' is to put money into financial schemes, shares, property or commercial ventures with the expectation of receiving a profit.

Basically, you're putting money into something, expecting to get money back. Sounds pretty simple.

We've all heard of someone touting their investments in some way. Whether that be your uncle talking about all the property he invested in back in the 1960s, or the crypto bro trying to turn a quick profit, or even your super fund sending you emails telling you how much your retirement fund has grown in value.

These are all types of investments in that the goal is to achieve a profit, whether it be through property, crypto, shares or something else. Some of these assets are a tad more risky, while others are less so.

But the goal with investing is usually the same: *to use your money to buy assets that make you more money.*

What is the stock market?

Stock market, stock exchange, equity market and shares market are basically all the same thing though there are slight differences between the stock market and the stock exchange.

The stock market is where you can access various exchanges, and exchanges are usually places where you can access a list of companies. For example, in the United States you can access the US stock market and in that market there are a variety of exchanges you can access, such as the New York Stock Exchange (NYSE) and the National Association of Securities Dealers Automated Quotations, better known as the NASDAQ.

In Australia, the stock/share markets mainly focus on the Australian Securities Exchange (ASX). (By the way, 'share' and 'stock' are the same thing: in Australia we usually use the term 'share', whereas elsewhere in the world the word 'stock' is used).

> *Fun fact: the first stock exchange was the London Stock Exchange, which began in a coffee house in 1773. It's evolved a lot since then with 60 exchanges now existing worldwide.*

So what exactly is the stock market?

The stock market is a secure and regulated environment where businesses can sell shares of their company. This allows companies to raise capital and individuals to have ownership through investments in the company.

A stock market is considered a secondary market, where shares are bought and sold from other investors, not directly from the companies themselves. Think of it like buying a car: you can buy directly from the dealer (primary market) or you can buy second hand from another person or third party (secondary market).

When shares are offered to the public for the first time, it happens through what's called an Initial Public Offering (IPO), which is part of a primary market. Once these IPO shares have been sold, you will be able to buy or sell them on an exchange — that is, the secondary market. In summary, you can't just go to Apple and ask to buy shares in the company; you'll need to buy them on an exchange.

On the US stock market, through the NASDAQ, you can buy and own a part of some big-name companies — such as Apple, Alphabet (Google) and Meta (Facebook) — and actually be a shareholder.

Meanwhile, on the Australian share market, through the ASX, you can buy and sell shares of companies such as Commonwealth Bank, Telstra and Woolworths.

In Australia, you can access some of the biggest exchanges and companies through a broker. Brokers facilitate the purchase and selling of securities. A security is a broad term that describes a financial instrument, and shares and bonds are different types of securities. Shares may also be referred to as stocks or equities. Buying any of these gives you part ownership of a company.

What is market fluctuation?

The thing about the stock market is that it moves up and down. The news and media hype up these fluctuations because that's what sells, but the truth is that market fluctuations are a normal part of the economic cycle.

Market fluctuation can be due to:

- *company performance.* Depending on the financial performance of a company, shareholders may act favourably (buying) or unfavourably (selling) towards shares, which can impact the share price

- *economic and industry trends.* If the economy or specific industry (let's say oil) is affected, this can impact the buying and selling of assets, resulting in market fluctuations

- *events and news.* Significant events (such as the 2022 Ukrainian war, which affected the cost of oil, wheat and other exports) can impact a market, affecting all aspects of the economy. This results in fluctuating markets. COVID brought about similar fluctuations

- *market sentiment.* Depending on the overall feeling about the economy and market, market sentiment can affect share prices. This is similar to how people talk about housing ('Now is a good time to buy as interest rates are low' vs 'Don't buy property now; there's an election around the corner'). Similar sentiments are applied to share investing — and sentiments vary according to people's optimistic or pessimistic feelings about the future

- *supply and demand.* This is another mechanism that can cause market fluctuations. For example, a negative sentiment can cause a fall in the markets due to an increase in the selling of shares, which leads to increased supply. This concept applies to all aspects of the economy, including housing, consumer items and even shares on the market.

For these reasons it's very difficult to predict what the market will do (who would have guessed that a pandemic would hit in 2020?). So it's advantageous to ignore all the fear-mongering that the media incites and just focus on what you can control, which is *how much* and *how often* you invest.

The interesting thing about market fluctuations is that historically the market usually recovers over the long term — even during events such as the tulip mania (when the cost of tulips sky-rocketed!) and the COVID dip — but it can be quite volatile and negative in the short term. Sometimes that correction takes a few months; other times it can take 10 years or longer. But it's important to remember that market fluctuation is an expected part of long-term investing. See figure 4.1 for an example.

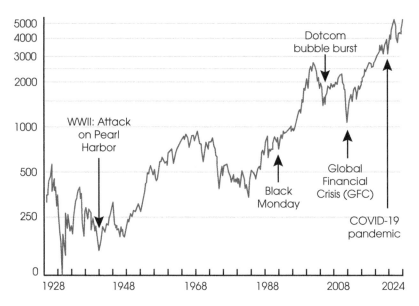

Figure 4.1: market fluctuation is a normal part of long-term investing

Source: Based on data from S&P 500 Index-90 Year Historical Chart. Macrotrends LLC. The S&P 500 Index® is a product of S&P Dow Jones Indices LLC. © S&P Dow Jones Indices LLC 2024. S&P®, S&P 500®, US500, The 500 are trademarks of S&P Financial Services LLC. Dow Jones® is a trademark of Dow Jones Trademark Holdings LLC.

Lessons from Japan

The Japanese market is a great reminder of the importance of diversification and spreading your investments across industries and sectors. Since its peak in the late 1980s, the Nikkei 225, Japan's main stock-market index, has struggled to reach those same peaks again, showing a long period of stagnation and slow recovery. This highlights the risk of overconcentration in a single market or asset class. Investors who allocated their portfolio heavily towards Japanese stocks during the peak of the market have experienced decades of underperformance, highlighting the need for diversification. This isn't to scare you away from investing! By spreading your investments across various geographic regions, industries and asset classes, you can mitigate the impact of a downturn in any single market, reducing your overall portfolio risk. It's a good reminder to not put all of your eggs into one basket.

What are asset classes?

An *asset* is something valuable or useful that a person owns. Conversely, in finance, *asset classes* refers to the various investment categories that you can invest in. These usually have similar characteristics and behave in a similar way.

The main asset classes are cash, bonds, shares, commodities, property and alternative investments.

Each of these assets has a different level of cost, risk, volatility, flexibility and tax implications. How you use them in your portfolio depends on your personal goals and circumstances.

Let's define each of them and provide a deeper explanation so that you can assess what might be best for your circumstances.

Cash

Cash is considered one of the safest investments because it is generally low risk (it's unlikely you'll lose the money you invest — your 'investment capital'), has low volatility and is secure (this is true for stable countries such as Australia, but less so in countries that have unstable governments and financial systems). With cash being low risk, it makes sense that saving cash in a savings account is a no-brainer, right?

Well, the thing with cash is that it's prone to losing its buying power because of inflation. As such, it's probably not a good idea to keep your money stashed under your mattress long term as it loses value over the years.

This is why it's often said that by investing your money you can keep up with inflation. However, like any asset, there's a time and place for cash. Cash is one of the most liquid assets, meaning it's easy to use and transact with. So, it's great to have some cash on hand as well. Incidentally, when we talk about cash, we don't just mean physical notes and coins. We're also referring to the cash in your transaction and savings accounts.

So, how do you invest in cash and when is it good to hold cash?

Cash investments are the money you have in a bank account, a term deposit or your piggy bank. In Australia, the government guarantees your money up to $250 000 through an authorised deposit-taking institution (ADI), meaning if an eligible bank goes bankrupt, you're still guaranteed up to that amount. This amount is per account holder, per ADI.

Investing in cash can provide a lot of flexibility because it's easy to access quickly and it's a good option when saving for short-term goals. Not only that, but investing in cash also reduces risk in your portfolio. You can use a high-interest savings account or an offset account (to offset your mortgage interest) as a way to invest in cash.

Some options for using cash to invest are to save for an emergency fund, to pay down debt, for short-term goals, to save for a downpayment on a property or to reduce risk in a portfolio.

Although cash is one of the safest asset classes, it is also the one that provides the lowest investment returns — for example, the average return of cash from 2012 to 2021 was 1.95 per cent. When you consider that the 10-year average inflation rate for the same time period was 1.97 per cent, the average real rate of return for cash was –0.02 per cent.

Cash is considered a defensive asset since holding cash can provide security and safety, but it won't make you rich as the returns are very low and often don't keep up with inflation.

Bonds

Bonds are also known as fixed interest, fixed income or debt securities. They are a form of lending where the investor loans money to an issuer — a government or company — in exchange for regular interest payments and the bond's face value when it reaches maturity (that is, when the agreed time frame of lending is up). Unlike shares, bonds are creditor investments offering a pre-determined return and typically less volatility. This is why they are considered a defensive asset and are usually held for 3 to 5 years with the risk being medium to low depending on who the loan is provided to (for example, lending to some governments is generally considered less risky than to a company). The safety and return of a bond depends on the credit-worthiness of the issuer, the safer the issuer, the lower the return offered. For example, bonds issued by the Australian government offer lower returns than those issued by Virgin Australia.

The benefit of bonds is that they can be quite flexible and liquid (if they have a secondary market), meaning they are usually easy to buy and sell and could be a good option for diversifying a portfolio to provide more stability. They have a slightly higher return than cash, but are also slightly riskier. However, bonds are considered a more stable investment than shares (which we will talk about next).

Bonds can also be purchased as an exchange traded fund (ETF) or a managed fund. In fact, you probably own some bonds in your super retirement fund.

As you get older, you may want to be more conservative with your investments. As their time frame for accessing money becomes shorter, many people consider investing in or increasing their allocation towards bonds.

Shares

Shares, also known as stocks or equities, are a piece of a company that you own directly or indirectly through a managed fund or exchange traded fund (ETF). When you buy shares, you physically own a part of a company. They are considered a growth asset (as it's assumed they will grow in value over time).

Unlike cash and bonds, shares are considered medium- to high-risk investments because there is no guarantee of dividends or returns on your investment and they have a high level of volatility, meaning the value of the asset will vary. Investments with a higher potential return come with greater variability in the investment value. Over the long term, returns are generally higher for shares than for cash or bonds, but shares are more volatile due to the constantly changing share price and because you can buy and sell shares easily (also referred to as 'liquidity').

Shares are a two-dimensional asset, meaning you can make money from them in two ways:

1. *dividends* — these are the regular income payments you receive from the company profits for being a shareholder (e.g. $1 a year annually for investing in the company)

2. *capital gains* — this is the difference between the price a share was initially bought for and the price it was sold for (e.g. if you buy a share for $10 and sell it for $15, then you've made a capital gain of $5).

So, using the dividend and capital gains example above, you would have a total return of $6 ($1 from dividends and $5 from the capital gains).

You can compare shares to an investment property in that dividends are similar to receiving rent on a property and both are considered an income payment. Capital gains comes into play when you sell the asset, which is similar to when you sell property (see figure 4.2). Remember, though, that both dividends and capital gains are taxed.

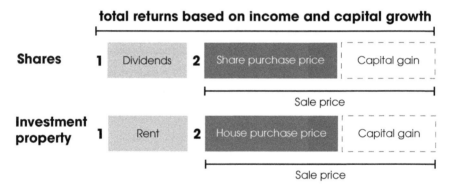

Figure 4.2: shares compared with an investment property

Where things get exciting, though, is that in Australia shares can come with a few tax advantages. If you've held an investment for over 12 months and have a capital gain, you may receive a capital gains tax (CGT) discount of 50 per cent, meaning you'll pay tax on only half of the capital gain for that investment. It's the government's way of rewarding you for investing long term! Using this example, if you've made a capital gain of $5, but you've owned the shares for over 12 months before selling them, you'll only pay tax on half the gain, $2.50 (the exact amount you'll be taxed depends on your marginal tax rate).

Furthermore, franking credits (which you'll read about in chapter 8) can also be advantageous tax-wise.

Shares are best suited to investors with a high risk tolerance and a longer time frame due to the market being volatile and usually needing time to recover from fluctuations.

ETFs (exchange traded funds)

You may have heard of exchange traded funds (ETFs), which generally hold a collection of stocks, bonds, commercial property or other securities in one fund. Think of them as a bundle as opposed to individual shares or bonds. In this section, we will mainly focus on ETFs that hold shares.

ETFs are a basket of shares that are bought and sold on the stock exchange and managed by a professional. They can either be active or passive and are bought through a broker. Active means that the fund manager is actively trying to beat the index's benchmark, whereas passive just tracks the index benchmark. Most ETFs are passive and track an index.

The chocolate analogy

Here's an easy way to think of ETFs.

You can buy individual chocolates or you can buy them in a box of different flavours. Buying individual shares is like buying individual chocolates, whereas buying a box of Favourites or Roses is like purchasing an ETF. The ETF holds all the different shares and you don't have to think about which one will perform well or not.

You can buy the chocolates from anywhere—Coles, Woolworths, Costco or even the petrol station. These different stores are like brokers. Some shops (or brokers) are cheaper, have better features or may be more convenient for your needs.

So, what does that mean?

Well, the ASX 200 is an index that tracks the 200 largest listed companies in Australia, and you can buy an ETF that tracks those exact 200 companies.

Two ETFs on the Australian Stock Exchange that track, and therefore hold, the 200 companies that are part of the ASX 200 are:

- *A200:* BetaShares Australia 200 ETF

- *IOZ:* iShares Core S&P/ASX 200 ETF.

The S&P 500, on the other hand, tracks the 500 largest listed companies in the United States. IVV (iShares Core S&P 500 ETF) is an ETF on the Australian Stock Exchange that tracks this index. Both of these passively track the largest companies through their respective indexes (or indices — same thing, just more jargon!).

The reason why so many investors opt for investing in low-cost diversified ETFs is because doing this involves very little maintenance. If a company drops from the top 200 Australian companies, it gets replaced, but the investor doesn't have to buy and sell or watch the market closely because all of this is done in the background, making it very passive for the investor. This essentially means, if you're investing in the top 200 companies, you'll always be investing in the top 200 companies, even if the actual companies change over the time of your investment.

For someone just starting to invest, an ETF is also a smart way to spread your money across many different companies. Imagine you want to invest in the top 200 listed companies in Australia (the ASX 200). Doing this directly would be very costly — about $100 000 — because you'd need to buy at least $500 worth of shares in each of these 200 companies. This is before you factor in the transaction costs or brokerage fees for 200 buys! However, with an ETF, you can start with just $500, or even less through micro-investing apps designed to dip your toes in and start learning. Diversified ETFs reduce risk, as you own a small part of a wide range of companies with just one simple investment.

ETFs vs index funds vs managed funds

'ETFs', 'index funds' and 'managed funds' are terms used to describe similar investments, but there are differences.

- *Exchange traded funds (ETFs)*. These are investment funds traded on a stock exchange. They work the same way as buying and selling an individual share. They offer a diversified portfolio that can track a specific index, sector, commodity or other assets but with real-time trading and price transparency. You buy ETFs through a broker.

- *Index funds.* These funds are designed to passively track an index. These can be EFTs or managed funds. Index funds are popular for their low-cost, passive investing strategy as they mirror an index rather than trying to outperform it.

- *Managed funds* (also referred to as mutual funds internationally). These are pooled investment funds managed by a professional fund manager who makes decisions on behalf of investors. These funds are not traded on an exchange and are valued at the end of each trading day based on their net asset value (NAV).

Buying our first ETFs

Tash: My first investment was $1000 in IVV, which is the iShares Core S&P 500 ETF (big thanks to my dad for the suggestion). This ETF invests in the largest 500 companies in the United States. I didn't completely understand why I was investing in this at the time but I just wanted to get started. I then continued trialling lots of different micro-investing apps and buying various different ETFs over the years. Now I just buy a few core ETFs and don't try to overcomplicate it.

Ana: When I first started investing, I knew that diversification was very important, so I did research on all the types of ETFs I thought I needed in my portfolio. I bought international, domestic (Canadian at the time), bonds, real estate investment trusts (REITs), emerging markets and high growth, among others.

Looking back I realise that I was nervous about buying the wrong type of ETF, so I bought them all (well, not all, but way too many!). I wish I had just bought one broad, low-cost diversified index fund instead. It would have simplified my portfolio, and I wouldn't have had so much overlap across the various sectors.

Now I invest in one or two ETFs regularly, knowing I can always adjust my investing portfolio as I learn more. I'm glad I got started investing, even if my portfolio held too many ETFs, because although I can buy more ETFs, what I can't do is buy time (which I lose more of the longer I procrastinate trying to perfect my strategy).

Property

Real estate is one of Australia's most popular asset classes. You can invest in real estate by purchasing a rental property such as an apartment, house or commercial property.

If buying physical property isn't your thing, there's also the option of buying a real estate investment trust (REIT) through the stock market. It basically functions as an ETF for properties.

There are two ways you can benefit from property investing: through rental income and through capital gains. It's similar to investing in shares. You receive a payment in the form of rental income and once you are ready to sell the property (provided it has gone up in value) you can also receive money from capital gains.

Investing in real estate has a medium to high risk as it depends on many factors, including the type of property (house vs apartment), its location and the tenancy risk (which occurs when a property is vacant and losing out on rent).

Although property may *seem* as though it doesn't fluctuate in value, it absolutely does — it just isn't as visible as shares. With shares you can see the price any moment of any day, but with property the valuation isn't as obvious.

Housing prices can fluctuate day by day depending on whether you make any modifications or whether there's less interest in the property area. But without a price tag that is constantly changing, it may *seem* as though property is less volatile.

Other risks that may be worth considering are fluctuations in mortgage interest rates, which can increase the financial burden of holding property, and even natural disasters such as flooding and fires can place a risk on this asset class.

Property is a higher risk asset than cash and bonds. However, this also means that there may be an expected higher return over the long run. Similarly to shares, property is a long-term investment since the cost to purchase real estate is high, with stamp duty, conveyancer fees and other upfront costs making it a more challenging asset class to get into initially.

But, like all asset classes, this may be one you'd consider for your own portfolio, which you will build based on your risk tolerance.

Figure 4.3 looks at investment risk and time frames as well as various asset classes in relation to risk and return.

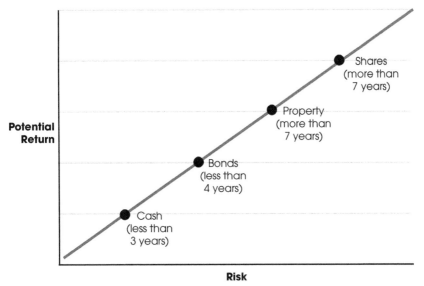

Note: The investment time horizon is the minimum time you should be willing to hold an asset to minimise your chances of financial loss.

Figure 4.3: various asset classes in relation to risk, return and time frames

Alternative investments

If cash, bonds, shares and property aren't enough for you and your investing strategy, you may be interested in alternative investments. These investments usually perform differently from the four main asset classes and have various characteristics — and they can be far riskier. Some are even classified as speculative, meaning it's a bit more of a guessing game as to how they will perform over time (and guessing whether they will go up in value).

So make no mistake, with alternative investments you are taking on more risk than with other investment assets. If you do choose to invest in them, consider doing so with money you are willing to risk losing — in case nothing comes from this venture. It's a good idea to only allocate a very small percentage of your portfolio (less than 10 per cent) to these investments.

Nonetheless, if you want to diversify your strategy, you may be interested in some of the following alternative options.

- *Infrastructure.* This includes transportation, power and telecommunications, which focus on building a support network. Opportunities to invest directly into infrastructure are usually reserved for large fund managers or super funds, and can include airports, toll roads, power plants and solar farms. The risk varies greatly depending on the investment. For example, Sydney airport is unlikely to disappear, so it would be considered low risk.

- *Venture capital.* There's the option to invest in smaller, non-listed companies that need funding to support operations and growth of the business. This is usually done through private equity firms and often requires a much higher minimum investment.

- *Collectables.* This includes investing in physical items such as artwork, Lego or Pokémon cards, which are deemed to go up in value in the long term.

- *Digital currencies.* This is a purchasing currency that exists in a digital form, such as Bitcoin.

- *Commodities.* These are basic goods and raw materials such as precious metals (gold, silver, platinum), base metals (copper, aluminium), energy (crude oil, coal, natural gas) and agricultural products (grains, livestock). Investors can directly own these products, buy commodity-specific ETFs or invest in companies involved in the production.

Although it's valuable to know about alternative options, we don't advocate investing in them unless you fully understand them and the risks. It's advisable to start with the four main asset classes first — cash, bonds, shares and property — before moving into this territory.

***

In part II of the book, we will discuss building your investing strategy. But before reading on, think about which asset classes you want to invest in and which you don't. All of them can be valuable depending on your life situation, circumstances and risk tolerance. To build a life that's financially secure, you need to take into consideration what your goals are, what you value and how you plan to get there.

Understanding how each asset class in your portfolio works is important for ensuring you're building wealth and creating a passive income stream so that you can build the life you love.

Make a start

Investing basics

- Write down all the different asset classes you own, and take note of any you would like to own in the future, or any you are not interested in investing in.

- Take a look at your super account, if you have one, and see what you're invested in. Take note of the asset classes and the percentages allocated to them.

- Look up a few different ETFs (share ETF, bond ETF and REIT) and see if you recognise any companies listed in them. Take note of the percentage allocated to that company within the ETF (this is also referred to as 'weighting').

Case Study

Jessica, 41

1. *Annual income*: 72k

2. *Source of income*: Customer service, no side hustle.

3. *Investing platform*:

   I started with Raiz and Spaceship. Once I was more confident I changed to CommSec for individual shares and Vanguard for ETFs.

4. *What do you currently invest in?* 40% shares and 60% property.

5. *What's the breakdown of your shares?* VAS 30 per cent, VDBA 40 per cent, VGS 30 per cent.

6. *How much do you invest and how often?* $700 per month.

7. *What are your money goals?*

   Being financially secure and building wealth. I want my children to grow up understanding money. I want to break the family history of living pay cheque to pay cheque. It's important to have my money work for me.

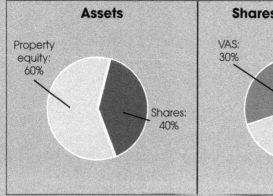

Assets

Property equity: 60%

Shares: 40%

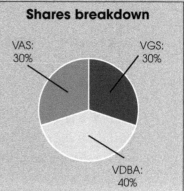

Shares breakdown

VAS: 30%

VGS: 30%

VDBA: 40%

8. *What's your biggest financial challenge?*

We live in Sydney ... enough said. I grew up with parents who would spend all their money each pay and not save. We had stuff but could never go on holidays or afford anything unexpected. I know it was a huge stress on my parents. When I became an adult I was worried I wouldn't have enough to live on. Once my kids were old enough, I was able to go back to work fulltime and actually earn a decent amount. I've been able to save and invest the increase of income and actively not fall into the trap of lifestyle creep.

9. *What's your investing strategy?*

I started with micro-investing and had some shares from previous employers. After listening to podcasts and reading about investing I became more confident about investing. I guess my strategy is to get into the property market and invest as much as I can to build a passive income. We aren't getting any younger and I would like my husband and I to start slowing down in 15 years or so.

10. *What's your biggest money mistake?*

Not starting sooner and getting a credit card just out of high school.

11. *Any advice for new investors?*

The right time to start is now, even if it's a small amount. It will grow — and compound interest is your best friend.

12. *How are you building a life you love through investing?*

I would say my plan is to build wealth for my family so we (my husband and I) don't need to work fulltime forever and enjoy the time we have with our kids and family.

Part II

Start investing

and build a life you love

Chapter 5

Build an investing strategy

Having an investing strategy is crucial if you want to remain focused on your investing journey and achieve your goals.

As you now know, investing is for the long term; therefore, if you don't have a strategy, it could be very easy to get tempted by things that don't align with your values. You might be more tempted to invest in things you don't fully understand, such as crypto, or non-fungible tokens (NFTs), or your friend's ambiguous start-up. Or perhaps you might get FOMO when there's a lot of media hype giving you a sense of urgency and tempting you to invest in things. You may well get nervous when the market dips for the first time since you started investing and you decide to cash out, selling all your shares and crystallising your losses.

That's why having an investing strategy is important. It keeps you focused on why you're investing, how long you're investing for, what your risk tolerance is and what exactly you're investing in.

The famous quote, 'If you fail to plan, you plan to fail' applies to investing too. So, let's make a plan together.

What to consider in an investing strategy

The best way to think about your investing strategy is to consider the following factors:

- risk tolerance

- asset allocation

- diversification

- time frame

- personal circumstances.

Let's take a minute to consider these.

Risk tolerance

Are you someone who needs a bit of security and stability in your investment strategy or someone who can totally deal with the fluctuations in the market? Understanding your risk tolerance will help you decide what percentage of your assets you want to hold in defensive (such as cash and bonds) vs growth (such as shares and property) assets.

Your risk tolerance may change over time too. If you have a long-term horizon you may have an appetite for more risk, knowing you can wait out market dips and corrections since you don't have to access your money anytime soon. However, if you're near retirement you may want to invest more money in low-risk assets because you don't want your investments to dip in value just when you're planning to sell some of them and retire. In this circumstance you may want less volatility and therefore have a lower risk tolerance.

Keep in mind that your risk tolerance will change during the course of your life. You may be willing to take more risks when you're young and single than when you have two kids to feed and a mortgage to pay off.

Since it's sometimes hard for new investors to actually know what their risk tolerance is, it's not a bad idea to trial micro-investing platforms (we talk about them in chapter 6), which allow you to invest small amounts. That way you can dip your toes in the water and see how you respond to market fluctuations.

If you feel anxious about seeing massive swings, you may consider a higher allocation towards defensive assets — for example, keeping more money in savings and only investing a small percentage into shares — until you become more confident. On the other hand, if you can happily tolerate the dips, you may be more comfortable allocating a higher percentage of your wealth towards higher risk investments (such as shares).

Asset allocation

What assets do you have in your portfolio and what percentage have you allocated to each asset class? Sometimes it's worth looking at your super fund to see how you're already invested (remember, super is for retirement, which usually has a long-term horizon, but it may give you an idea of how to think about your asset allocation).

By considering what percentage you want each asset — such as cash, bonds and real estate — to hold, you can ensure that you're comfortable with the balance (also known as the 'weighting') of each. Assets such as cash and bonds have a lower volatility and therefore are lower risk than shares and property.

Diversification

Instead of putting all your eggs in one basket, diversifying your portfolio allows you to include various sectors to ensure you have eggs in *lots* of baskets! You can diversify by country — e.g. Australia, the United States — or international markets. You can also invest in different sectors and industries, such as technology, finance and infrastructure. Or, you can diversify based on the size of companies, which are classified as 'large-cap' (large, well-established companies), 'mid-cap' (smaller, stable companies) or 'small-cap' (smaller companies). For the most part, you'll probably hold a diverse portfolio with at least large-cap companies in it. And, of course, you can diversify your asset classes (cash, bonds, shares, property), which we alluded to in chapter 4.

In case something were to happen to the market in one area (let's say there's volatility in the US tech sector), at least you are invested in other countries and industries, making the investing ride less bumpy and therefore less risky.

> *Diversification is the reason we love ETFs! It makes it easy to invest in different countries, sectors and even assets by buying one or a few ETFs.*

Time frame

Your investing goals may be drastically different if you are saving to buy a house in 3 years vs planning for retirement in 30 years. Knowing your time frame can help you determine the best strategy to use to reach those individual goals.

For short-term goals, perhaps investing in shares is too volatile; putting your savings into cash may be more suitable. As for long-term goals, perhaps cash is too conservative and investing in shares or property makes more sense. Only you know your time frame and what strategy is best for you.

It's worth checking in every few years to see if you're on track to reach your goals as things can change and you will need to adjust your portfolio accordingly.

Personal circumstances

As we've seen, the financial goals you had in your 20s are likely to differ from the goals you have in your 40s or 60s. Life happens and goals change. You may buy a house, combine finances with a partner, have a kid, receive an inheritance, lose a job or win the lottery. Each of these circumstances can drastically change the way you view your goals.

It's okay to change your strategy — many of us do over time. One thing to remember, though, is that if something drastic happens (for example, you receive an inheritance after the death of a loved one), it might be best to wait 6 months or so and not make any impulsive financial decisions. Allow for time to pass and think clearly about how the occurrence fits into your strategy. Ideally, you'd like your strategy to have a long-term focus, even if it includes some short-term goals.

Our investment strategies

 Ana: Over the years my investing strategy has changed. At first I was all about reaching FI by increasing my income and investing as much as possible. But after the birth of my first child, security and buying a home became a priority.

Now my strategy is growing my wealth, paying down a home loan and having a variety of income streams. My goal is to have flexibility so that I can spend time with my kids while they are young while also doing meaningful work and taking up passion projects.

It's interesting to see how my strategy has changed over the years, including shifting to more ethical investments. I'm focusing on building wealth without compromising my values.

 Tash: I was really excited about the idea of travelling, and this helped me build good saving habits early on. I would work lots, save, travel during uni breaks and then come back and repeat. I always knew that I wanted to invest because I was lucky enough to grow up in a household that spoke about money openly. As with Ana, my initial interest was in the FI movement, but after having a bit of a break (and moving states to work at a ski resort for a few snow seasons), I realised that I really enjoyed working and didn't want to retire early and do nothing at all. I still like the idea of FI and having choices, but I am no longer super frugal or working towards retiring as early as possible.

Investing strategy in practice

You now have an idea of what you should have in your portfolio and how to juggle various considerations, including risk, diversification and time frames. But how will you keep track of it all? *drum roll please* This is where you build your investing strategy!

An investing strategy is a blueprint of what you need to do to achieve your goal. For example, if you have a goal to run a marathon, you may have a plan to run 3 days a week. Sure, there are other things you can do, like eat more healthily and get more rest. But it's important to run for at least 3 days to prepare and build your body up for the big race.

Building an investing strategy is similar. There are things you can do along the way to reach your goals more quickly, but if you don't have habits and plans in place, you may not reach your goal at the ideal time.

So much of investing is about habit building and behaviour. In many cases, building the habits (or better yet, automating them!) can keep you on track.

So, what are some of the strategies you can use? There's a bunch! Let's delve into them! (And remember, you're not limited to picking only one of the following strategies — some can work together.)

Timing the market

We've all heard the saying 'buy low and sell high' whereby investors try to time the market and get the best price for their shares. It sounds great in theory, but unless you have a crystal ball, it's really hard to beat the market and get a better return than simply investing in a diversified ETF.

One of the challenges of timing the market is that additional tax considerations will come into play if you're trying to make a quick win (for example, you may have to pay the full 100 per cent capital gains tax instead of getting the 50 per cent discount if you hold for 12 months).

Although it may be fun to try to time the market, we don't recommend it as a strategy for beginners (or, in fact, for most people), but it is worth mentioning because this strategy gets talked about a lot.

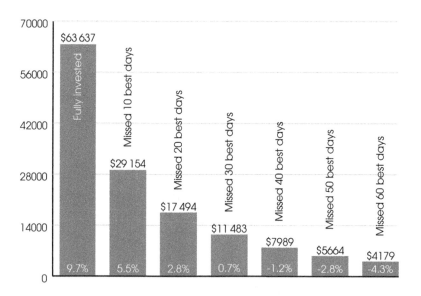

Figure 5.1: returns on a $10 000 initial investment based on missing out on the best days in the market from 1 January 2004 to 29 December 2023

Source: Copyright © 2024 JPMorgan Chase & Co., All rights reserved

Figure 5.1 shows the impact of missing some of the best days of the S&P 500 on a $10 000 initial investment. If you were buying, selling and then buying again but missed only 10 of the best days of returns in the 20-year period shown, the value of your portfolio would halve.

Unfortunately, no-one can predict the future. By pulling your money out and missing some of the best days for returns, your portfolio can be severely impacted.

Dollar-cost averaging

This is a favourite strategy of many long-term investors. That's because it takes the guess-work out of 'timing the market' and focuses more on investing in a regular cadence. The benefit of dollar-cost averaging (DCA) is that you invest a fixed amount of money at regular intervals, regardless of the share price, meaning you are continuing to grow your wealth irrespective of what the market is doing.

By doing this, your regular fixed investment buys more shares when the price is low and fewer shares when the price is high, which can help reduce the impact of volatility on your portfolio and provide you with an average price over time. Take a look at figure 5.2 (overleaf) for an illustrative example of why dollar-cost averaging can be so beneficial.

Lump-sum investing

Lump-sum investing involves investing a large sum of cash all at once, rather than spreading it out over time. This approach can be valuable if you want to get into the market quickly instead of over a period of time (such as with dollar-cost averaging) or you believe that the market is undervalued and you want to take advantage of the low prices.

Figure 5.2: how dollar-cost averaging works

This strategy may be advantageous if you have a large amount of money from selling a property, getting an inheritance or winning the lotto (wishful thinking!) that you want to invest or if you just want to get into the market.

In fact, *Morningstar* research shows that on a 10-year average, 9 out of 10 times lump-sum investing can be a better strategy than dollar-cost averaging. But if you don't feel comfortable investing a large amount at once, or are concerned about making the wrong choice, then dollar-cost averaging into the market might be the best option for you. Remember that with personal finance there's the mathematical answer and then there's the emotional answer, and both play a part in decision making!

Buy and hold

This strategy is a popular one with long-term investors, and it is pretty self-explanatory. Investors buy an investment and hold it for a long period of time. The idea behind this strategy is that over the long term, the investment will hopefully increase in value, despite short-term fluctuations in the market.

The goal of this strategy is to invest in well-established companies that have a long history of profitability, pay dividends and tend to be less affected by market fluctuations.

This strategy doesn't eliminate risk as there's always a possibility of losing money during a market downturn, but it does focus on long-term investing, which we advocate for as well.

Dividend investing

Dividend investing involves investing in companies that pay dividends, which are regular payments to shareholders. Dividend-paying shares or ETFs can provide a steady stream of income and can be a good option for investors looking for a passive investment strategy that is focused on income. It's important to note that dividends can be volatile as they depend on a company making a profit, which is then paid out to shareholders. Some years profits are better than others, so dividend payouts are subject to change.

Here's an example.

If you invest $10 000 in an ETF that has a 4-per cent dividend return each year, you'll receive $400 in dividends.

Accordingly, $100 000 = $4000 in dividends, and $1 000 000 = $40 000 in dividends.

While $400 might not sound like enough to quit your job for, it is a step towards your journey of either supplementing or replacing your 9–5 working income. The magic of dividends is that you don't need to sell your shares to get paid dividends — your shares will hopefully continue to grow while you earn a nice passive income.

Keep in mind that dividends are taxed, so depending on your marginal tax rate (also referred to as your personal tax rate — it's the threshold you're taxed at based on a percentage of your income) this may not be as advantageous as focusing on capital growth investing, which invests in ETFs that aim for growth in value rather than dividends. Remember that CGT discount we mentioned? It makes capital growth more attractive to investors earning a higher income than to those nearing or in retirement.

Index investing

You've probably heard people say, 'Keep it simple and buy index funds' if you've been floating around the personal finance space. So what is an index fund? Let's recap.

Index funds buy shares following the rules of an index. For example, the ASX 200, which is an index of the top 200 companies listed on the Australian Stock Exchange; or the S&P 500, which invests in the top 500 US companies. By investing in an index, you gain exposure to a diverse range of companies and sectors, which can help to reduce risk. This is a very common strategy that long-term investors abide by when buying ETFs.

Ethical investing

ESG investing, which is often referred to as ethical investing, stands for environmental, social and governance investing. This strategy concentrates on investing in companies that have strong sustainability or ethical practices. This can include companies that have a positive impact on the environment, promote social equality or have good governance practices.

ESG investing can be somewhat controversial. For example, if a company has strong environmental practices but its products are manufactured in sub-par conditions that exploit employees it's hard to determine whether the company falls under the ESG title. In fact, it's beneficial to look at the list of companies under an ETF to see if they align with your own values.

What you consider ethical may be different from what someone else considers ethical. Plus, there are various ways to invest ethically, such as through an ESG ETF. Some examples are:

- *VETH*: Vanguard Ethically Conscious Australian Shares

- *ETHI*: BetaShares Global Sustainability Leaders

- *VESG*: Vanguard Ethically Conscious International Shares Index

- *ESGI*: VanEck MSCI International Sustainable Equity

- *FAIR*: Betashares Australian Sustainability Leaders.

Although ESG investing may not be perfect, being aware of where you are investing and intentional of what companies you invest in can make a difference.

Passive vs active investing

Passive investing involves investing in an index fund that mirrors the performance of that index without the need to select individual shares or time the market. This can result in average returns.

Active investing, on the other hand, involves picking companies and shares that you expect will outperform the market or index over time. This approach usually involves investing through a fund or manager that actively (hence the name 'active') manages the portfolio by making buy and sell decisions.

Now, why would you want to invest in an active vs a passive ETF?

Well, it mainly depends on your goal and risk tolerance.

There are usually higher fees associated with active ETFs because active funds need to pay someone to closely track the companies in order to make educated decisions on who they believe will outperform the index. This may be of interest to someone who wants to specifically be more involved, is trying to beat the index or wants to invest in a particular area such as ESG investing, where active management may provide more value and therefore the higher fees are justified.

It is worth noting that the ASX website has stated that more than 80 per cent of Australian fund managers underperformed the index over a period of 15 years. In the United States, 92 per cent delivered lower returns than the S&P 500 index (which is usually used as the benchmark for investing).

In fact, the world's most famous investor, Warren Buffett, made a million-dollar bet with fund managers that over a 10-year period they wouldn't be able to outperform the S&P 500 inclusive of fees. Sure enough, he was right, demonstrating that passive investing wins out long term.

Day trading

Day trading involves actively buying and selling shares in the short term with the aim of capitalising on short-term changes in price. The goal is to buy low and sell high, thereby making money as quickly as possible.

Those involved in day trading often borrow or leverage capital (meaning they use debt to buy and sell) in order to purchase additional assets. This can come with a large risk because the trader needs to have a strong understanding of the market, companies and currency to make a profit.

What's more, there is often a cost in the form of a brokerage fee that comes with buying and selling, and you likely won't benefit from the CGT discount.

Day trading is not something we recommend, but we wanted to mention it because it's often talked about.

What we invest in

 Ana: My strategy is to keep things as simple as possible. That's why I invest in low-cost diversified passive index funds.

When I first started investing, I wanted to get into the market as soon as possible and invested a lump sum. I then continued to invest by dollar-cost averaging into the market. To date, I have only ever sold one share (of an individual company), effectively making me a long-term, buy-and-hold investor.

Over the past few years I've only invested in ESG funds, which aligns with my values, as I want to be more intentional about how I spend and invest my money. I also automate my investments so that I don't have to think about them, thereby building wealth without much effort (although I had to put a pause on investing while I was on parental leave due to not having an income).

Even though my strategy has changed a bit over the years, I like to be as hands-off as possible when it comes to my investments so that I can focus on more important things like my family and passion projects.

 Tash: While I enjoy learning about personal finance, I don't want to spend every day reading the news and monitoring my investments. I want investing to be a stress-free thing that happens in the background, which is why I buy and hold index-tracking ETFs over the long term. I have one property that is now an investment and might look to buy a second one in the future, but for now I prefer the freedom of having an easy-to-manage mortgage while investing extra funds into ETFs. Investing doesn't have to involve watching the markets every day — nor should it be like a clip out of *The Wolf of Wall Street*. You can just set and forget.

What strategy should you use?

As we've seen, strategies can change over time depending on your risk tolerance, assets, goals and timeline, so it's okay to change things around as needed. In fact, it would be strange if your investing strategy in your 20s was the same as your strategy in your 50s.

For most, investing is a means to building a life you want for yourself. It can give you the financial backing to do things you otherwise wouldn't be able to do, like start a business, go back to school or take a year off to road trip with your family.

Remember, investing is a long and slow process, and your strategy will help keep you on track. You need to have a clear strategy and goal in mind to keep yourself motivated for the long term. It's important to be clear on your goals and what you are hoping to achieve, and to know how to use the information you have at your disposal to make the best decision for yourself at any particular time.

Your goals will change, and that's okay too. Remember, the best way to learn is by trying. No-one becomes a professional surfer in one day; it takes time and dedication to get confident in a skill. The same goes for investing.

Invest your own way

Everyone's financial situation and strategy will be different. Here are a few realistic scenarios of people considering their own goals and strategies as they embark on their investing journey.

Jo and Sam

Jo and Sam are both 30 years old. They have a mortgage on their home and both have steady jobs. They have a surplus cash flow of $1000 per month and want to invest this money for the long term (for retirement), but also to be able to access their money if they need to. They don't have any short-term goals that would require access to their investments. They are also comfortable with the idea that their investments might decrease in value in the short term.

Jo and Sam are long-term investors and can therefore ride out and recover from market volatility in the short term. As they are comfortable with market volatility, they choose to invest using a high-growth, high-risk strategy (90 per cent+ of money into growth assets such as shares). They would like to prioritise higher long-term average returns over capital stability in the short term.

Jo and Sam should speak to a financial adviser because they may have the potential to convert their home loan to a deductible debt over the long term using a method known as 'debt recycling'. Debt recycling involves using the equity in an existing asset (such as property) to invest in income-producing assets (such as shares), aiming to convert non-deductible debt into tax-deductible debt while gradually paying down the original debt.

Zoe

Zoe is 32. She is renting and has a steady job. She currently has $100000 saved and can save around $10000 per year. Her short-term goal is to purchase a unit for around $600000 in the next 3–5 years, and she is considering her investment options.

As she will probably need at least a 20 per cent deposit (plus costs) for a loan, she will need to save at least another $20 000 before she buys a unit in the next 3–5 years. Based on her current savings capacity, her goal is likely to be achievable. She could look at investing her money, but even a conservative risk profile will come with the risk of volatility and there would be no guarantee of a positive investment return in the short term.

Zoe decides to prioritise capital stability over potentially higher returns so that she can be sure she will have all of her savings when she's ready to buy. That way she can continue using her higher interest savings account, which she has compared to options with other banks, and is satisfied she's getting a competitive interest rate.

Jules and Jay

Jules and Jay are both 45 years old. They have recently received an inheritance. They don't have any intention of using this money now, but plan to potentially renovate their home 8–10 years from now. They are willing to take on some investment risk but are worried about significant volatility (such as their investment dropping 10 per cent or more in the short term).

Jules and Jay have a long-term investment time frame but some aversion to being exposed to significant volatility. Though their time frame indicates that they could invest in a high-risk, high-volatility portfolio, they want to take a more moderate approach (half their money in growth assets such as shares, and the other half in defensive assets such as savings accounts and bonds). They understand that this risk profile comes with the risk of negative returns/volatility, but they are satisfied that the likely risk is a level they are comfortable with.

Goal setting

We know that goal setting is good, but you might be wondering if you can skip this step ... Unfortunately the answer is no. Your investing goals will determine what you invest in, which assets you pick and which platform is suitable for you so it's an important part of your investing strategy. We'll say it again: personal finance is personal and there's no one-size-fits-all solution. But stick with us and you'll know how to invest by the end of this book.

If you don't know what you want to do and why, it's hard to work out how to get there. That's where SMART goals come in.

SMART goals

There are a few different frameworks for setting goals, and you need to find one that works for you. We are going to teach you how to create SMART investing goals, which will keep you accountable and make it easier to achieve your goal.

SMART stands for:

- **S**pecific

- **M**easurable

- **A**chievable

- **R**elevant

- **T**ime frame.

Here's what each means.

Specific

Have you ever set a vague goal — something like 'I want to invest' or 'I want to save'? Now is the time to get clear. Do you want to invest for financial freedom, to buy a house or to quit your job? Be very specific about why you are investing and for what purpose. The more specific, the better. Saying you are 'saving for my future' is less motivating and harder to measure than 'saving for a deposit on a house to live in'.

Measurable

Most investing goals are easy to measure because they involve numbers. Having actual numbers you are working towards can help you measure your success and even calculate the percentage of the goal you've already achieved. For example, your goal might include needing to save a 20 per cent deposit for a $600 000 house, which means you need to save $120 000. This is measurable because you can track how much you've saved towards that deposit.

Achievable

You need to set achievable goals to be successful. It can be tempting to set nice, dreamy goals, but unless they're realistic ones that are achievable you may be setting yourself up for failure. For example, you may have a goal to invest $50 000 in a year. But is that realistic?

Are you able to save and invest $4167 a month, or $962 a week? Or do you need to adjust the amount or time frame? Perhaps saving $10 000 for the year or having a timeline of three years is more achievable.

The last thing you want to do is set an unrealistic goal that will in turn set you up for failure.

The flip side of this is that your goal is too easy to achieve and therefore you aren't pushing yourself enough. Only you can know the answer to these questions.

Relevant

How relevant is your goal? This step is all about deciding if your goal is something you want and something that aligns with your values.

Let's use our house deposit goal as an example. Do you actually want to buy a house? Or is this something you think you should be doing because your parents told you to. If it's the latter, chances are you won't be motivated to work towards it.

Knowing your 'why' will help you understand your values and the purpose of your goals. Really think about how this goal can enable you to live a life that you want. Perhaps that house is exactly what you dream of because you've always wanted a place to call your own. Figuring out your 'why' and your goal's relevance is important for keeping you on track.

Time frame

Make sure your goal has a time frame. This will keep you accountable. Investing $10 000 in one year or $10 000 in 10 years are two very different scenarios. Parkinson's law also applies here: your work will expand to fill the time allotted for its completion. This is why having a time frame, or deadline, will keep you focused on your goal.

Having a specific time frame also helps with motivation and ensures you can look back and reflect on whether you accomplished a goal or not.

Plus, it's always fun to celebrate the goals you did achieve!

Examples of SMART goals include:

- *saving for a house.* I will save $60 000 for a 20 per cent deposit on a $300 000 property by contributing $1000 per month for 5 years

- *investing for retirement.* I will invest $100 per week for 40 years to reach my goal of having $1 000 000 invested to fund my retirement

- *emergency fund.* I will build an emergency fund of $15 000, which is equivalent to 6 months of my living expenses, by transferring $500 from each monthly pay into a savings account. I will reach $15 000 in 2.5 years.

Short- vs long-term goals

Short-term goals in the finance world are usually ones that are achievable within one year. They can include things like saving or investing for:

- a holiday

- school fees

- a car

- an emergency fund.

Long-term goals are generally 5–7+ years in the making. Examples of longer-term goals are:

- investing to retire

- purchasing a property to live in

- saving to pay for your kids to go to a private high school.

Your goals and time horizon will depend on whether saving or investing is best for that goal. Remember that investing can be volatile because the market fluctuates, so you want to make sure your money is invested for a longer period of time. Short-term goals require less volatility so saving may be a better alternative to investing to guarantee your money is stable.

Remember that personal finance decisions don't exist in a bubble — there are lots of factors to consider. As you get older and your wealth grows, your finances may become more complex, so careful consideration is important. Alternatively, you can always talk to a financial advisor.

Deciding between paying off a mortgage or investing

As we remarked on in chapter 2, a common conundrum is 'Should I pay off my mortgage or invest?'

There's no right answer as to whether you should pay off your mortgage or invest. The best you can do is take everything into consideration and find out what works for you.

A lot of this depends on your goals and risk tolerance. It's definitely not an easy question to answer, but it's an important one when you're considering your investment strategy, so we're going to talk a bit more about it here.

Note that in this section we are mainly discussing a principal place of residence (PPOR). Investment properties (IPs) have additional tax considerations.

Here are some of the things to consider when deciding whether to pay off a mortgage or invest:

- mortgage interest rates vs investment returns

- debt recycling

- concentration risk.

Mortgage interest rates vs investment returns

The first consideration when debating the two options is looking at the interest rate.

If you have a high interest rate, it may make sense to pay off your mortgage as quickly as possible. This is because you'll be saving a lot of money in interest payments over the life of your loan.

In February 2024, the average mortgage interest rate was 6.84 per cent per annum, according to *Mozo*. The average annual return on shares is historically 7–10 per cent per year. As these returns are quite similar, it may make sense to pay off your mortgage. By paying off your mortgage you would effectively be saving yourself money (which is tax free!).

However, if you have a low interest rate, it may be advantageous to invest your money instead because you could potentially earn a higher return on your investments than you're paying in interest on your mortgage.

It's also worth considering whether you have a fixed or variable loan. With a fixed loan, you have the security of knowing your interest rate won't fluctuate, and therefore you could consider how investing fits within your budget. Some fixed-interest loans may have restrictions or repayment penalties hindering you from paying off more than the required amount.

A variable loan, on the other hand, may result in unforeseen interest rate rises, which can result in financial strain. When you're deciding between paying off your loan or investing you need to account for mortgage stress.

Most variable interest rates allow extra repayments via an offset or redraw facility. Using one of these can reduce the interest rate owed on a loan, saving you money in the long run, while also providing you with easy access to cash in case you change your mind and decide to invest, or need the money in an emergency.

Although we don't know what the future market returns are, weighing the differences in interest rates, mortgage types and investing returns is a consideration.

Keep in mind that you'll need to pay tax on your investment earnings. Returns on investments also aren't guaranteed, while paying off your mortgage will be a guaranteed return in the form of savings.

Debt recycling

Debt recycling is a strategy that involves using equity in your home (i.e. the value of your house minus your mortgage) to invest in an income-generating asset (such as shares).

This approach aims to reduce non-deductible debt (mortgage) while increasing tax-deductible debt (investment loan). This option may be advantageous for those looking for a tax-advantaged strategy while paying off their house and investing at the same time.

Debt recycling can be a complex strategy that you might need support to set up. It's best to chat to a financial advisor if this is something you're considering.

Concentration risk

Another factor to consider is concentration risk.

We've discussed the value of diversifying your investments. The same goes for property. If your goal is to pay off your mortgage, you may need to consider your need for diversification. If your home loses value, you could lose a significant amount of money. By spreading your investments across various asset classes, you are minimising your risk and the impact of a single investment's poor performance in your overall portfolio.

***

So, you can see that having an investment strategy is an important step towards building a life you love and one that gives you financial security. In the next chapter we'll talk about all the ins and outs of investing, which will give you the tools you need to set up your own portfolio.

Make a start

Building an investing strategy

- Consider your asset allocation. Do you think it is aligned with your risk tolerance? Are your assets diversified enough?

- Complete a risk-tolerance quiz online and see how the results align with your current or potential investments.

- When looking at the investing strategies outlined in this chapter, is there one (or a few) that aligns with how you

(continued)

want to invest? If so, write it down to hold yourself accountable. For example, if you want to dollar-cost average, write down the amount you want to invest and what the regular interval will be (e.g. $50 a week).

- Write down your SMART investing goals. What time frame do you have for each, and what is the best asset to invest in for your given goal? Bonus points if you can also include an investing strategy within your goal.

Case Study

Renee, 25

1. *Annual income:* $55 000

2. *Source of income:* assistant editor for film and TV and freelance video editor.

3. *How do you budget your finances?*

   I allow myself a portion of what I've earned during the week so that there is always something left over to cover me if I get sick or don't have work for a bit. So, for example, I might earn $1600 one week, but will only pay myself $800 as a salary. Then, another week, I'll only earn $600, but I can then continue to pay myself $800 so that nothing feels dramatically different in my day to day. That $800 is then split into $430 for bills (all regular bills added up for a year, divided by 52 and then divided by 2 so it's split between myself and my partner), $81 for investing, $50 for my emergency fund, $150 in savings for a house deposit and the leftovers for spending.

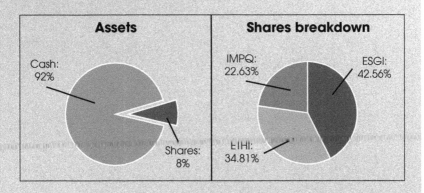

Assets	Shares breakdown
Cash: 92%	IMPQ: 22.63%
Shares: 8%	ESGI: 42.56%
	EIHI: 34.81%

4. *What do you currently invest in?*

   92 per cent cash, 8 per cent ETFs.

5. *What's the breakdown of your shares?*

   ESGI 42.56%, ETHI 34.81%, IMPQ 22.63%.

6. *How much do you invest and how often?* $81 per week.

7. *Which broker/platform do you invest with?* Pearler.

8. *What are your money goals?*

   I invest for the security of having the money to fall back on in 10, 20, 30 years. I don't have a specific goal in mind just yet but the general feeling I have as I invest is that this money could be used to supplement my income in future if I decide to cut down on work or start a family.

9. *Why did you start investing?*

   Listening to *The Broke Generation* I heard the host mention that investing was a good thing to do, but she wasn't able to go into any detail. It all seemed very overwhelming. Then I saw the *Get Rich Slow Club* podcast recommended on Instagram, listened to a few episodes and decided to give it a crack!

10. *How much debt do you have?*

    HECS debt, around $30 000. It was less when I graduated but then indexation happened. ☺

11. *What's your biggest financial challenge?*

    Mainly the challenge of starting my financial journey from 0. A lot of my friends received money from their parents when they turned 18 and have been able to grow that to buy a house etc. My family didn't do this for me, and also had pretty bad spending habits so I've had to unlearn a lot of things.

12. *What's your investing strategy?*

Invest in ethical ETFs that align with what I believe in, but still keep a large portion of my savings invested in cash. The strategy has changed in that there was no strategy or investing in ETFs until recently.

13. *What's your biggest money mistake?*

Not thinking about ways to organise my freelance income and just compiling it all into one account (minus tax — I was good at keeping that separate). Now I don't let myself use it all. Some gets kept in another account as if it's holiday/sick pay since I don't get paid those benefits.

Chapter 6

How to invest and what to invest in

By now we're sure you'll agree that passive income is essential for building a life you love. The more passive income you make, the less time you need to spend working. Since time is finite, wouldn't you rather spend it doing something other than working in an office? Of course you would!

Even if you love your job, having passive income provides you with security and flexibility. Ultimately, having freedom and opportunity to create a fulfilling life is what we all want.

Now that you know all about how the share market works and how to apply your investing goals and strategies, let's put that into practice and learn how to actually invest in the share market.

In this chapter we'll take you through the steps to follow when you're deciding how much and how often to invest, and help you pick a platform to invest through. We've also included some example investment portfolios created with help from financial advisors at Guideway Wealth.

Let's get started!

What is a broker?

Traditionally, a broker was a person you hired to manage your investments. They acted as a 'middle man', buying and selling stocks on behalf of investors for a fee known as a brokerage fee.

Today, the role of brokers has evolved. While traditional brokerage firms do still exist, many people have turned to apps and online brokers or execution intermediaries (sometimes referred to as trading platforms). These platforms offer a convenient and accessible way to buy, sell and manage your investments.

What are brokerage fees?

Whether you are using a traditional broker or an investing app, there will be fees involved. These fees can vary widely and are either a fixed fee or a percentage of the overall purchase price. They are usually charged for buying and selling shares and ETFs.

Investment apps often market themselves as low-cost brokers— with some even having zero brokerage trades (a 'trade' is what happens when you buy and sell)—but they may still charge fees for account maintenance, inactivity, foreign exchange, transaction fees, or earn a rebate by grouping your shares with other investors (as they'll get a better deal for the large trade). It's important to be aware of these fees as they can quickly add up over time.

Deciding what to invest in

With your investing goals sorted, it's time to decide where to invest your money. This will depend on your time frame and risk tolerance, which we discussed previously. Let's look at deciding what to invest in, in relation to goals.

For short-term goals of less than a year, it's usually safest to put your money into a savings account. That way you can earn interest and your money is safe.

For medium-to-longer term goals, it can be harder to decide whether to invest in something with a higher level of risk, such as shares, or something with a lower level of risk, such as cash or bonds. Which option you pick depends on your risk tolerance and how flexible your plan is. For example, if you want to save to buy a house and you choose to invest in shares, what will you do if you're ready to purchase but the market is in a downturn? Would you be willing to wait out the volatile time or would you rather cash out your investments at a loss? Investing in shares comes with a higher level of risk, but also has the potential for higher returns (although these are never guaranteed). Cash is safer, but it doesn't have the same potential for higher returns. Therefore, it's important to consider your goals and the asset class associated with them.

Market crashes are a normal part of investing and it's wise to expect and plan for these. If your goal has a fixed and short timeline, placing your money in a savings account or term deposit may be the wisest choice to ensure it's not only available when you need it but also protected against any loss of money. If you can be flexible with your timeline (and you can delay purchasing that house for a few years), then investing in shares may be an option for you. The goal is to avoid having to sell your shares when the market is down.

A longer-term goal could be focusing on retiring or FI, which is the idea of living off your passive income. If you won't need that money for a long time, investing in something like shares might be a good option. Long-term investing obviously requires a long-term horizon: the longer your timeline, the lower the risk because you can ride out the market corrections and not sell when the market is down or volatile.

Knowing your timeline, risk tolerance and what your goals actually are will help you decide what to invest in.

Deciding how much you want to invest

To get started, you'll need to decide how much you want to invest and pick an investing platform. It's important to work out the amount you want to invest before deciding which investment option and platform are best for you.

Do you want to invest $5 a week or a one-time lump sum of $10 000? Are you just investing whatever is left in your bank account at the end of the month or being diligent about saving, say, $1000 every 2 months for investing?

The amount you want to invest impacts which brokerage platform you can invest through. Some brokers let you invest in micro-amounts — like $5 dollars — whereas others require you to invest $500 at a minimum. Once you know how much you can invest, it's worth calculating how frequently you should invest based on the cost of the brokerage fees. Remember, you get charged a brokerage fee per trade (i.e. per transaction), so knowing the optimal frequency is valuable in keeping your costs low.

A general rule of thumb is to try to keep fees under 1 per cent of your trade amount. Fees can have a big impact on your investment returns, especially for smaller investment amounts.

We'll illustrate this with an example.

Investment amount: $200

Brokerage fee: $10

Total cost: $200 (investment) + $10 (brokerage) = $210

That means you are paying 5 per cent for your brokerage fee ($10 is 5 per cent of $200.).

Your $200 investment will need to grow from $200 to $210 to make the money back that you paid in fees, before you start getting a return. This means your investment needs to grow by 5 per cent before your returns will actually be making you money. This is significant when average annual returns range from 7–10 per cent for shares.

Now, there's a caveat to this: sometimes fees for smaller investments can be seen as the cost of learning — meaning it's better to at least start and get in the market to see how you go than to wait until you have a large enough amount to invest. It's difficult to know how you'll react to market fluctuations if you've never experienced them before, which is why starting to invest early is often beneficial.

You can use an online investment frequency calculator like the one illustrated in figure 6.1 (overleaf) to find out how to minimise your brokerage fees. Figure 6.2 (overleaf) presents an optimal investment schedule.

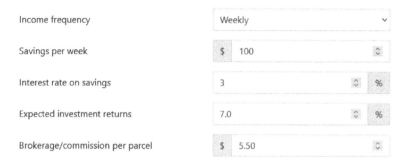

Figure 6.1: use an investment frequency calculator to figure out the optimal frequency to invest at
Source: © 2024 Stack Exchange Inc

Optimal investment schedule:

Invest $1204 once every 12 weeks.
This amount includes the brokerage fee and $4 interest.

Approx. total Invested ($) after 10 years

Every week	$70 198
Every 6 weeks	$73 470
Every 12 weeks	$73 649

Figure 6.2: an example investment schedule
Source: © 2024 Stack Exchange Inc.

Choosing an investing platform

In Australia, investing platforms such as brokers or investing apps may offer one, two or all three models of buying and selling shares. The three models are:

- CHESS-Sponsored

- custodial

- micro-investing.

Knowing the differences between these models is important when deciding which platform is best for you. Make sure to always read the product disclosure statement (PDS) and target market determinations (TMD) before signing up. Take the time to do your research, read reviews and check whether the platform has had any issues with the Australian Securities Investment Commission (ASIC).

CHESS-Sponsored

CHESS stands for Clearing House Electronic Subregister System, which essentially means that you directly own your shares and they are tracked on an external platform called a share registry. When you start investing, the ASX issues you a personal Holder Identification Number (HIN). Your HIN identifies you as the owner of your shares. When talking about CHESS-Sponsored shares, we simply mean an investing platform that offers you your own HIN.

The CHESS system is unique to Australia, so if you were to purchase international shares these would likely be under a custodial arrangement dependent on the jurisdiction, where there are specific controls or protections based on how common custodial ownership is.

Pros of CHESS-Sponsored shares:

- *Direct ownership of your investments.* If an investing platform closes down for any reason, it is clear that you are the owner of your shares and you are able to transfer to another broker or sell them through the associated share registry.

- *Simple to transfer.* It's simple to transfer these shares either via an Off Market Transfer or a Broker to Broker HIN transfer to a new investing platform. You may wish to do this if the fees to buy and/or sell change, or if you find a platform that better meets your needs.

Cons of CHESS-Sponsored shares:

- *Higher brokerage fees.* Whilst fees change often, when looking at the investing platforms offering CHESS-Sponsored shares vs those with custodial ownership in general, the per-trade fees for CHESS-Sponsored shares are often higher. At the time of writing, per-trade fees on CHESS-Sponsored shares start from $3 an investment, with some platforms offering them free under certain amounts; but, they typically range from $5.50 to around $20 for transactions under around $15 000. You will generally be charged a brokerage fee every time you buy or sell a share.

- *Higher minimum investment.* The minimum amount required to buy shares is usually $500.

- *Only whole shares are available.* You can't buy part of a share (known as a fractional share) using the CHESS-Sponsored model. So if you want to invest $750 and each share costs $100, you would only be able to invest $700.

Examples of investing platforms offering CHESS-Sponsored shares:

- Pearler

- SelfWealth

- CommSec

- Stake

- NAB Trade.

Custodial

With the Custodial Model, shares are held on your behalf by a custodian, which is usually the financial institution you're investing through. You won't be issued your own HIN. Instead, the broker will likely hold and track everyone's investment under one HIN – referred to as an Omnibus HIN, meaning you will have indirect ownership of your shares. You may see resources online that indicate custodial platforms are CHESS-Sponsored, which is true in the sense that they may hold their client assets on an Omnibus HIN which is one HIN for all clients — however, this is a little different to the common or casual understanding, where CHESS-Sponsored is used to imply an individual HIN. An SRN (Securityholder Reference Number) is used to identify the owner of shares that are held by a share registry (i.e. the shares are issuer sponsored).

Pros of the custodial model:

- *Lower minimum investment amount.* As the cost to buy shares is often cheaper, or even free, these brokers can offer a lower minimum amount — from 1 cent to $100. Outside Australia, the custodian model can allow for fractional share investing, meaning you can buy part of a share. This is dependent on the financial firm and differs widely.

- *Cheaper brokerage fees.* Pooled investments under one HIN may mean lower costs for brokers and cheaper fees for users.

- *Less paperwork and consolidated tax reporting.* As you aren't the direct owner registered for the shares, the custodian will manage some of the paperwork for you. They usually provide you with annual tax reports or summaries.

- *Access to other markets.* The custodian model is a more widely used model, so you are able to buy shares on US or other overseas markets.

Cons of the custodial model:

- *Commingled ownership.* If an investing platform goes bankrupt, closes for any reason or has major disruptions to its operations, getting your money or assets back can be a little murky or take relatively extended periods of time.

- *Less transparency.* While some may state they have 'free brokerage', this may not apply to all types or trades or they could charge other fees such as cash account management fees or foreign exchange fees. Or, in some cases, may group your trade to make money (which can be disadvantageous as the trade may not be processed instantaneously.)

- *Transferring can be complicated.* Not only complicated, but with some platforms transferring may not be an option at all! Not being able to transfer to another broker means your only option would be to sell and potentially trigger capital gains tax.

Examples of custodial investing platforms:

- Superhero

- Vanguard Personal Investor

- Sharesies.

Micro-investing

Micro-investing is as it sounds: investing small or 'micro' amounts. It involves buying units of a managed fund. The fund pools everyone's money together and invests it on behalf of the group. Instead of owning shares directly, you own units — which represent a percentage — of a pool of money. That pool of money is invested by a fund manager in a diversified portfolio of assets.

Micro-investing can be a beneficial way to invest if you only have a small amount to invest or if you want to start small to get used to the volatility that comes with investing.

Pros of micro-investing:

- *Good for learning.* Micro-investing apps usually have low minimum investments, such as 1 cent or $5. It's hard to find out how you will react to things like market crashes without having some skin in the game and experiencing it. Micro-investing allows you to start investing with small amounts so you can learn as you go and get more comfortable with investing and market fluctuations.

- *Lower minimums.* When micro-investing, you can usually start with just $5. (Traditional brokers or investing platforms often have a minimum investment amount ranging from $100 to $500.) Plus, you need to consider the impact of brokerage fees on your returns and ensure you are investing enough in each share parcel to make the brokerage fee worth it. (The general rule is to keep brokerage fees under 1 per cent of the transaction cost.)

- *Less paperwork and consolidated tax reporting.* The goal of micro-investing apps is to make investing easy and accessible. As you don't own the shares directly, you are spared the paperwork involved in CHESS-Sponsored ownership. Micro-investing apps often offer a tax report or summary. Some may even tell you which columns on the ATO website to put each number into when reporting your investment earnings at tax time.

- *Good for building habits and automating.* Micro-investing apps are a good way to start automating your investing and to build the habit. Just as with exercise, you need to make a consistent and ongoing change when investing, and micro-investing apps make this easy to do. Remember that investing even $5 a day can quickly add up.

Cons of micro-investing:

- *Ongoing management fees.* Instead of paying a one-off brokerage fee, you'll often pay an ongoing management fee. While this may work out better for small investment amounts or short-term time frames, you'll need to work out what will be more cost effective in the longer term if you plan on holding your investments for 10, 20 or 30+ years.

- *No direct ownership.* Similarly to the custodian model, with micro-investing, you don't have direct ownership of your shares. Therefore, if the company collapses, getting your money back can be a bit murky.

- *Limited options.* Micro-investing apps usually have three to eight investment options. (This can also be seen as a pro because it helps to reduce analysis paralysis and keeps investing simple. It is also easier to avoid the distractions of the latest 'hot' penny stock.)

- *Can't be transferred without triggering a sale and potential capital gains.* At the time of writing, only Raiz offers the option of transferring out, with some terms and conditions. The other micro-investing apps don't currently allow transfers. This makes it harder to change brokers as your investment strategy and plan develops, with the only option being to stay and continue paying ongoing management fees or sell and be subject to capital gains tax.

- *Can't transfer to your own HIN.* If your strategy changes and you want to invest in assets under your own HIN but don't have a minimum of $500 to invest, you may want to save in a high-interest savings account until you have enough money, and then start investing in ETFs.

Examples of micro-investing platforms:

- Pearler micro

- Raiz

- Spaceship.

Other considerations

As we've established, there are a lot of investing platforms to choose from. It can be overwhelming to look at them all. You can always sign up to a few and see what suits your needs.

Remember the chocolate analogy, where we discussed buying chocolate as a single bar or a box? It's important to keep in mind that *what* you buy matters more than *where* you buy it from — that goes for both chocolate and ETFs. Many platforms hold the same shares and ETFs, as depicted in figure 6.3.

	Varieties		Where to buy	How to choose?
Chocolate	Bar	Mixed box	Supermarkets, service stations	What works best for you.
Shares	Shares	ETFs	Brokers, apps, in-person	

Figure 6.3: the chocolate analogy

There are a few things to look at when choosing a broker. The trick is to find a broker that works for you and has features that you value.

Here are some considerations:

- *Fees.* Compare and calculate the brokerage fees, foreign exchange fees, ongoing management fees and cash account fees. Brokers' fee structures and prices vary. Find one that seems reasonable to you.

- *Available investments.* What do you want to buy and can you buy it on that platform? For example, Vanguard Personal Investor offers access to all ASX listed investments, but the free brokerage only applies to Vanguard ETFs. Do you want to buy only ASX listed shares, or are you looking to buy ones listed on other exchanges too?

- *User interface and ease of use.* Is the platform easy to use or too complicated? If you prefer an app on your phone, is this available? Do you need live data or a set-up that is more passive and long-term focused?

- *Account types.* What type of account do you need: individual, trust, joint or minor? If you're considering investing for a child, Ana discusses investing options in her other book, *Kids Ain't Cheap.*

- *Minimum investment amount.* What's the minimum you can invest on the platform? Does the amount work for you, or were you hoping to invest smaller amounts?

- *Withdrawal options.* How much are the fees to sell and can you transfer shares to another brokerage platform?

- *Deposit options.* Can you deposit from any bank account or do you need to open a new one? For example, at the time of writing, CommSec Pocket requires a Commbank account, which may come with fees unless you meet certain conditions. Are there options for instant transfers or will transfers take a few days? Does this matter to you?

- *Tax-reporting tools or integrations.* Does the platform offer tax reporting or does it integrate with a tool such as Navexa or Sharesight?

- *Automation capabilities.* If your priority is to invest at a regular cadence, it may be worth considering what platform has automation tools that can automate your investing in the same way as you automate paying your bills. This can provide you with ease of mind and reduce any friction from continually investing.

- *Education and support.* Some platforms have educational tools that help teach you about investing, allow you to see other people's portfolios or returns, or help you with goal setting. Depending on what capabilities you are looking for, this may be important. Seeing another person's portfolio can be helpful as a starting point for your research, but copying it isn't recommended and can be risky. Make sure you understand the asset, the risk and the recommended time frames before deciding to invest.

Making an investment

The requirements for making an investment (or placing a trade) differ depending on the broker. With some brokers, you'll need to put in the number of shares that you want to buy, but with others (such as Pearler), you can put in the total cash amount you want to invest and they will work it out for you.

Let's use the Vanguard Australian Shares (VAS) Index ETF as an example. To find the price of each individual share, you can google 'VAS ETF' or find it on your broker's website. They usually have live share pricing.

For this example, we found the share price of 98.84 AUD for VAS on Google on 01/04/2024.

> *If you had $500 to invest, you could buy five shares (500 divided by 98.84 = 5.06). Unfortunately, you can't buy fractional shares on the ASX, so with $500, you'll be able to buy five VAS shares for a total of $494.20.*

> *If you want to buy six shares (98.84 × 6), it will cost $593.04.*

Market vs limit orders

When purchasing shares, you have a choice of placing a market order or a limit order.

A market order is an instruction to buy or sell shares as quickly as possible at the market price. This type of order is usually instant and secures the best possible price, meaning there is no price certainty. Market orders are common for highly liquid shares (shares that are easy to sell) where the price doesn't fluctuate significantly in a short time frame. This makes them a good option for buying regular ETFs.

A limit order is an instruction to buy or sell shares at a specific price, or better. The execution of this order is not guaranteed. It only occurs if the share price hits the specified limit. This offers price certainty, but it may not happen at all. Limit orders are more commonly used for selling less liquid shares and for investors who are stock picking and concerned with shorter term gains.

For long-term investors, particularly those buying index-tracking ETFs, market orders are generally the more appropriate choice.

Terms you may come across

The financial industry can make things sound complex by using financial jargon and brokers often follow suit.

To help with making sense of the jargon, here are some terms you might come across when buying shares and what they mean:

- *quantity*: the number of shares or units of an ETF that you are wanting to buy or sell

- *units*: often used in reference to a managed fund or ETF, a unit represents a portion of ownership in a fund. When you invest in an ETF, you are buying units of that fund

- *ticker code*: this is a unique series of 3–4 letters, kind of like an acronym, that represents a particular share or ETF. It's a quick way to identify a specific equity

For example, the ticker code for Apple Inc. is AAPL. You may also see it as NASDAQ: AAPL, where the stock exchange is listed first

- *value*: the total worth of the transaction — that is, the number of shares multiplied by the price of each share

- *conditional*: an advanced type of share order that occurs only when certain conditions, set by the investor, are met. For example, price, volume or other market changes

- *expires*: when placing a limit or conditional order, 'expires' refers to the date or time when the order will no longer be valid if it hasn't been executed

- *GTC (good till cancelled)*: a type of order that remains active until it is either executed or cancelled. It doesn't expire at the end of the trading day

- *day only*: an order that is valid for the current trading day only.

Automation

As you know, the magic of compound interest works wonderfully when you consistently add to and grow your investments.

Have you ever set a goal to eat better, go to the gym or start running? Did you do it once and then never again? Or did you make it a habit, build it into your routine and stick to it?

Long-term investing works best when it's a consistent habit. If you could automate a task and save time, why wouldn't you? By automating things, you are buying yourself time. Time to do the things you love and, in turn, create a happier life — which is what we're all about!

Automating is great because it allows you to:

- *invest consistently and build the habit.* This is key to the dollar-cost averaging strategy

- *emotionally detach.* This reduces the risk of making emotionally driven decisions such as impulse buying when things seem good or panic selling during market downturns

- *save time.* Once you've set up the automation, you will save all the time involved in transferring money across, logging into your brokerage account, looking for something to buy, potentially being distracted by other options and then placing the trade

- *cost efficiency.* You can set up an automation plan that makes the most of your brokerage fees. Pearler, for example, has an automation option where you can direct debit a regular amount and then arrange for your accumulated funds not to be invested until they reach a certain amount. For example, you could direct debit $200 per fortnight and have it automatically invest when the total amount reaches $1000.

How we automate

 Ana: I used to track everything and do it manually. It helped me feel like I was in control of my money. But once I had a handle on everything and knew exactly how much I was spending and saving, it made sense for me to automate all my bill payments, savings and of course, investments.

I would set up my account to invest on the day I got paid—that way I knew I was paying myself first and growing my wealth.

Tash: Automated investing options are the best invention! I used to enjoy tinkering with my investments a little too much—every time I logged on to buy another parcel of ETFs, I'd get distracted by other options. Eventually, I set up automated investing on Pearler and it has saved me a lot of time, and helped me stick to the plan.

How to automate

There are two options for automating.

One way is to automate a direct debit into your brokerage account and then set up a reminder to manually invest once it reaches the amount you want in your share parcel.

The other way is to find a broker that allows you to fully optimise the process. Pearler was one of the first platforms to offer automation for CHESS-Sponsored shares. Similarly, most micro-investing apps offer some form of automation.

Here's how to automate:

1. Set your investing goal. Make sure it's a SMART goal!

2. Pick a platform (don't get stuck on this — you can always change your mind later. Remember: *what* you buy matters more than *where* you buy it).

3. Go to an investment frequency calculator and find the optimal frequency to invest.

4. Use the information from the calculator to set up your automation.

5. Set and forget!

So what should I buy?

Now that we've dipped into types of investments, goals and brokers, you might be wondering what to invest in. We'll get into that next.

But before we talk about what to buy and inspect some example portfolios, here are a few important reminders.

- *Don't forget about your goals and their time frames.*
  Unless you have a decent cash buffer and cash funds
  to cover any short- to medium-term goals (e.g. deposit
  for a home; renovations; holiday), don't invest. Save
  first. Investing (even in a relatively conservative
  portfolio) comes with various risks, including that
  there is no guarantee that your investment will
  experience a positive return (especially in the
  short term).

- *Keep it simple.* A lot of people over-complicate their
  investment strategy. Don't do this unless you have
  complex needs, in which case you should definitely be
  seeking professional advice. In most cases, a simple
  index ETF portfolio will perform better over the long
  term than trying to pick winners (this is backed up by
  research).

- *Time in the market is more important than timing
  the market.* Invest consistently over time instead of
  moving in and out of the market/investments. You'll
  never consistently pick the top and the bottom of
  every market cycle. Develop good investing habits that
  allow you to dollar-cost average into the market. This
  means that even a declining market will benefit you

because you will be buying investments at lower prices (decreasing your average cost), which will benefit you long term.

- *Past returns are not necessarily indicative of future returns.* Recent negative returns do not mean that an investment is not investment worthy. Likewise, high positive returns do not mean that an investment is investment worthy.

- *Keep costs low.* As well as the management fees charged by the fund manager, you'll also likely be up for brokerage/transaction fees from a broker/platform. This is because you need a broker or an investment platform in order to purchase an ETF. You should shop around to reduce the costs of your transactions. This is particularly important if you are buying regularly because the brokerage fees will add up over time and eat into your total returns.

Example portfolios

Not sure where to start? The portfolios outlined in table 6.1 are examples of how to set up simple portfolios of ETFs that are low cost and diversified across index investments. You could use any one of these as a base and adjust it to meet your needs. The specific products mentioned should not be taken as personal recommendations or as an indication that the product is appropriate for you. You will need to consider whether the products are right for you based on your circumstances, and contact a financial advisor if you think you need assistance or personalised recommendations. And, as we've said before, you should also refer to the product disclosure statement (PDS) and target market determination (TMD) documents for each of the products for more information.

Table 6.1: examples of simple, low-cost, diversified portfolios

Investing style	Safe	Conservative	Moderate volatility tolerance	High volatility tolerance	Very high volatility tolerance
Investments to research first	High-interest savings accounts	Vanguard Diversified Conservative Index ETF: ASX code VDCO	Vanguard Diversified Balanced Index ETF: ASX code VDBA	Vanguard Diversified Growth Index ETF: ASX code VDGR	Vanguard Diversified High Growth Index ETF: ASX code VDHG
Minimum investment time horizon	No minimum	4–5 years	5–6 years	7 years	8 years
How much money is invested in growth assets (shares)?	0 per cent	Around 30 per cent	Around 50 per cent	Around 70 per cent	Around 90 per cent
How has this performed historically (over the past 10 years)?*	Depends on your bank ☺	4.58 per cent per annum	6.22 per cent per annum	7.85 per cent per annum	9.45 per cent per annum
How has this performed historically (over the past 5 years)?*	Depends on your bank ☺	2.64 per cent per annum	4.21 per cent per annum	5.93 per cent per annum	7.61 per cent per annum

* Past performance is not a reliable indicator of future returns. Returns assume reinvestment of all income distributions, after Vanguard management fees. Vanguard managed fund counterparts to the ETF portfolios have been used for 10-year returns as the ETF portfolios have not been around for 10 years. Returns as at 30 June 2023.

Source: vanguard.com.au.

Understanding minimum investment time horizons

Think of your investment journey similar to building your career. When you start your career in your early 20s, you don't expect to reach the peak immediately. It takes years of different experiences — some good, some challenging — to grow professionally. You might change jobs, learn new skills or even face setbacks such as job losses or a difficult project. But over time, these experiences contribute to your overall career growth and success.

Similarly, when you invest, think of it as a long-term career path for your money. Just like your career, investments don't grow steadily and predictably all the time. There will be periods of rapid growth (just as there might be a promotion or successful project) and times of decline or stagnation (like an unsuccessful job application or a tough period at work).

Setting a minimum investment time horizon of, say, 7 years or longer is like committing to a career plan. It allows your investments time to experience various market conditions — good and bad — and ultimately grow over the long term. Just as you wouldn't abandon your career after a tough year, staying invested for the long term allows you to work through the rough patches and take advantage of the growth periods.

So, just like you're building your career with a long-term perspective, approach your investments with the same mindset. It's about steady growth, learning from the ups and downs and staying committed to your long-term goals.

Understanding volatility in simple terms

We've referred to the term 'volatility' several times in this book, but what exactly is it? You can think of volatility as how much the value of your investments go up and down over time. Imagine it as a boat in the ocean: the rougher the sea (higher volatility), the more the boat will rock. If the sea is calm (lower volatility), the boat moves smoothly.

When you invest in something with higher risk, such as shares or property, you can expect more ups and downs — this is higher volatility. Why do people choose these bumpy investments? Because over a long time, they tend to give better rewards than safer options such as bonds or keeping your money in a savings account. It's like choosing a boat that rocks a lot but can take you to more exciting places.

The idea is, if you're going to take the risk of being in a boat that rocks more, you'd want a better reward for it, right? That's what happens with these investments. The bigger the waves you're willing to ride out, the more you could potentially earn in the long run.

Factors to consider

When deciding on which ETFs to invest in, the main factors to consider are:

- *management fees*. Most index ETFs will have a management fee of between 0.00 per cent and 0.50 per cent. Lower fees may mean that the ETF will more closely track the underlying index (i.e. it will have a lower tracking error, which is the difference between the ETF performance and the performance of the index that the ETF is attempting to track)

- *the target index*. It's possible that two different ETF products investing in the same asset class will track two different indexes and therefore experience different performance. For example, VAS tracks the ASX 300 (the 300 largest companies in Australia), whereas IOZ iShares Core S&P/ASX 200 ETF tracks the ASX 200 (the 200 largest companies in Australia). With some asset classes, indexes will vary greatly. With others, they will be very similar (e.g. the ASX 300 and the ASX 200 are very similar, but some international share indexes can have larger variations)

- *liquidity*. An important metric when looking at ETFs (or managed funds) is the fund size (measured in dollars or funds under management). Generally, the bigger a fund is, the easier it's going to be to sell your investment. The example funds listed in table 6.2 are all sufficiently large to provide good liquidity (that is, the ability to buy or sell) at the time of writing. If you're looking at other options, be mindful of the size of the fund as your investment in a smaller fund may be more difficult to sell

- *currency hedging*. For international investments, you'll need to decide whether to currency hedge or not. Currency hedging is a method used to protect against losses caused by fluctuations in exchange rates when dealing with foreign currencies. Buying an AUD hedged ETF means that the fund manager will minimise the impact of changes in foreign currency relative to AUD (e.g. changes in the AUD/USD exchange rate). Sometimes hedging will have a positive impact on returns (when the AUD strengthens) and sometimes it will have a negative impact on returns (when the AUD weakens). As with investment markets, it's not possible to predict future changes in exchange rates. Diversified ETFs (like VDHG) may have a predetermined currency hedge range.

How currency fluctuations can affect you

Imagine you're in Australia and planning a dream holiday to the US next year. You're saving up for all the fun stuff you'll do there — visiting theme parks, exploring cities, enjoying great meals. But there's a catch: the exchange rate between the Australian dollar (AUD) and the US dollar (USD) keeps changing. If the AUD weakens against the USD by the time you go on your holiday, you'll need more AUD to get the same amount of USD, making your holiday more expensive. The opposite is also true, if the AUD strengthens, your holiday becomes cheaper.

DIY investment options

If you're looking to construct your own portfolio of high-quality index investments, take a look at the ETF options for the asset classes in table 6.2 (overleaf).

Just a reminder that Vanguard, Betashares and iShares are all fund managers. They create and manage ETFs, some of which are listed in table 6.2. You can find out more about an ETF by googling its ticker code. For example, the ticker code for the Vanguard Australian Shares Index ETF is VAS.

Table 6.2: DIY investment options

Australian shares	International shares (unhedged)	International shares (hedged)	Bonds	Cash
Vanguard Australian Shares Index ETF (VAS)	Vanguard MSCI Index International Shares ETF (VGS)	Vanguard MSCI Index International Shares (Hedged) ETF (VGAD)	Vanguard Australian Fixed Interest Index ETF (VAF)	High-interest savings accounts or term deposits
iShares Core S&P/ASX 200 ETF (IOZ)	iShares Core MSCI World ex Australia ESG ETF (IWLD)	iShares Core MSCI World ex Australia ESG (AUD Hedged) ETF (IHWL)	iShares Core Composite Bond ETF (IAF)	iShares Core Cash ETF (BILL) *
Betashares Australia 200 ETF (A200)	Betashares Global Shares ETF (BGBL)	Betashares Global Shares Currency Hedged ETF (HGBL)	Betashares Australian Composite Bond ETF (OZBD)	Betashares Australian High Interest Cash ETF (AAA)*

* Cash ETFs can be useful in some circumstances, but generally you will be able to achieve greater interest rates by shopping around for high-interest savings accounts or term deposits with banks directly. Additionally, deposits with an authorised deposit-taking institution (ADI) (banks, building societies or credit unions) are government guaranteed up to $250 000 per account holder, per ADI. Investments in cash ETFs are not covered under this scheme and therefore carry slightly higher risk.

Investing mistakes to avoid

In the world of finance and investing, small mistakes can end up costing you a lot over time. While you don't want to get caught up trying to avoid making mistakes completely (they are a normal part of the journey), here are some of the most common ones to avoid.

Owning the same companies by buying overlapping ETFs

VDHG, VAS and A200 are all popular ETFs, so should you buy them all? Beginner investors often have analysis paralysis when it comes to investing, thinking 'buying all is better than buying one'. In fact, we thought the same way and ended up with too many ETFs in our own portfolios.

However, it's valuable to look at which companies are held within the ETFs to see if they contain any of the same companies. While it isn't the end of the world if you buy overlapping ETFs — you'll just have a higher allocation to a particular region or industry than you originally thought — it's an important consideration when investing over the longer term.

To compare the overlap between ETFs, you'll need to look at what they invest in and what shares or funds they hold.

For example, VAS and A200 are Australian-focused ETFs, whereas VDHG is a diversified ETF that has exposure to Australia as well as other international markets, bonds and fixed interest.

VAS and A200 have the biggest overlap. VAS tracks the ASX300 (largest 300 companies on the ASX), and A200 tracks the ASX 200 (largest 200 companies on the ASX).

VDHG has a 35.77 per cent allocation to Australian equities at the time of writing, so by buying VAS and A200, you would be increasing this allocation. This isn't necessarily wrong or a bad thing; it just depends on whether it aligns with your investment plan. Is there a reason for wanting to have a higher allocation to Australian shares?

Buying things you don't understand

Have you ever heard someone talk about the next hot stock, watched a TikTok about the next crypto going to the moon or seen someone on social media encourage you to get into the next big thing before it's too late? It can be tempting, but investing in things that you don't understand can be a mistake for a number of reasons.

- *Not being able to evaluate risk and returns without fully understanding the asset.* It's hard to consider the risks, possible returns, how to mitigate these and whether or not they fit into your investing plan.

- *Vulnerability to scams.* Unfortunately, the investment world is full of scammers, and a lack of understanding makes it easy for scammers to exploit people with their complex and too-good-to-be-true schemes.

- *Emotional decision making.* Without a solid understanding of why you're investing and whether the returns you're expecting are reasonable, it's easy to make emotionally driven decisions.

- *Panic selling.* You might panic and sell during a market downturn if you don't understand why you're investing in something.

    An example of this was the dot-com bubble. During the late 1990s, there was a rush of investments into internet companies, many of which lacked solid business models and plans. A lot of people put money into these companies without understanding the tech sector and the feasibility of these businesses. When the bubble burst, many companies failed and there were significant losses for investors who had blindly invested their money.

Investing in what you understand is of fundamental importance. It helps you make informed decisions, manage risks and find investments that are aligned with your financial goals. This is why it's recommended that you do your own research.

Not rebalancing your portfolio

Leaving your portfolio to its own devices as it grows can be a mistake because this can also lead to an asset allocation that no longer aligns with your intended investment strategy, risk tolerances and financial goals. It can result in a portfolio that's heavily overweighted to an industry that is doing well in the short term, but that may not serve you in the longer term.

Going back to the dot-com bubble, those investors who had a balanced portfolio in the early 2000s would have ended up with a significant allocation towards tech stocks as these would have grown faster than others in their portfolio. If they did not rebalance before the dot-com bubble burst, the overexposure to tech stocks could have led to substantial losses when the sector crashed.

Rebalancing is when you realign the asset allocation within your investment portfolio to bring it back to your desired allocation. Typically, this is done by buying or selling assets within the portfolio.

For example, if you're getting closer to retirement, you may be less risk averse and want to hold more defensive assets such as cash and bonds.

When rebalancing your portfolio, it's important to remember that transaction costs (brokerage fees) and CGT implications will apply.

Regular rebalancing is key for managing your portfolio and ensures that your investing strategy stays on track, aligns with your goals and risk tolerance, and adapts to changing market conditions. By not rebalancing, you may be exposing your portfolio to unnecessary risk and smaller returns.

One of the benefits of diversified ETFs such as VDGR and VDHG is that rebalancing happens within the fund.

Setting unrealistic expectations

Having unrealistic expectations can lead to poor decision making, increased risk-taking and potential (or very likely) disappointment. Unrealistic expectations can come from a lack of understanding, overconfidence or being influenced by stories from friends, family, reddit forums or social media.

Following are some common expectations.

- *High returns in the short term.* Markets can be volatile and unpredictable in the short term, and expecting high returns is often unrealistic. Achieving high returns also involves taking excessive risks, which can lead to significant losses.

- *Assuming there will only be positive returns.* A common mistake is to underestimate risk and the possibility of a downturn and consequently to not be prepared for it.

- *Overconfidence.* Some investors believe they are able to time the market and pick stocks, which has proven to be very difficult, even for professionals.

Investing isn't a get-rich-quick scheme; it's actually a slow and long process. Understanding the realistic returns and how volatile the market can be is something worth grappling with when choosing your allocation of assets — especially around defensive vs growth assets.

Not talking about money

How does talking about money make you feel? Often, money can be seen as a taboo topic that is rude to talk about, but we should all talk about money more. The 'keeping up with the Joneses' phenomenon can have a big impact, but you don't know the truth of someone's financial life until you peek under the surface. In fact, talking about money can be both illuminating and a chance to learn new things.

There are a few reasons why.

- *Opportunities for learning.* Conversations around money can be educational. You can learn about how others are doing things and why. It can also be good to get different perspectives on the various ways of managing and viewing finances.

- *Financial taboos.* Not talking about money continues the idea that money is a taboo topic, which can lead to increasing the financial literacy gap.

- *Money can be stressful.* Talking about it with others can help alleviate stress.

Having regular money conversations can increase financial literacy for you, your family and friends, while also creating a support network as you navigate financial decisions. Plus, talking about money can provide you with information that can arm you for your next salary negotiation, request for mortgage rate reduction, or even just finding the best savings rate for your emergency fund. In fact, talking about money can be empowering.

Not understanding the tax implications of selling

This is a big one. There's the saying 'buy low and sell high', but really, we should add a whole caveat about how if you sell, you should talk to your accountant or financial planner as it can have a massive impact on your taxes.

Although you do receive a 50 per cent capital gains discount on shares held longer than 12 months, there's still planning that needs to be done around when you sell and how that will impact your taxes. Remember, any returns earned from selling shares will be included in your taxable income, which means they may impact the tax bracket you're in or any subsidy you might be receiving from the government (such as paid parental leave or child-care subsidies).

Similarly, if you're planning to sell at a loss, it may be smart to talk to a tax accountant to plan the best time to do so.

Not starting

The biggest investing mistake we see is people procrastinating and just not starting to invest. The opportunity cost of not investing can be huge.

Our mistakes

 Ana: I was planning on travelling for a year and saved up a large amount of money. I was worried it wouldn't be enough, so I sold some shares (this was in a tax-free savings account—TFSN—in Canada). I never ended up using the cash from the proceeds of the shares, and in fact, they sat in a savings account for years.

I'm embarrassed to say that I lost out on potential gains due to my money just sitting in cash not earning any interest because I'd been lazy.

 Tash: I view most of the 'mistakes' I made along the way as the cost of learning, but one big one stands out whenever I reflect on my investing journey. I decided to buy an ETF called BBOZ when the market first crashed in 2020 during the pandemic. Lockdowns were ongoing, vaccines weren't available and the future was really uncertain. Surely the market wouldn't recover?

I was wrong. BBOZ is an inverse leveraged ETF, which meant that every time the market recovered by 1, I lost 2. This ETF used leverage, which means gains, but also losses, are magnified. This was my first attempt at betting against the market rather than just buying low-cost index-tracking ETFs. I lost between $4000 and $5000, and while I know that I should have just stuck to my original strategy, I'm glad I learned the lesson early on. Despite overwhelmingly negative headlines, the market still recovered quickly, and it's a good reminder that no-one can accurately predict the future.

Make a start

How to invest and what to invest in

- Pick a broker and open an account. This is the first step to investing.

- Use an investment frequency calculator to figure out how much you should invest and how frequently.

- Pick one ETF that aligns with your goals, strategy and risk tolerance and invest in it. Remember, you can always change your strategy in the future if needed.

- Automate your investing. Make it as simple as possible so that you can set and forget.

Case Study

May, 37

1. *Annual income:* $153k + super.

2. *What do you currently invest in?*

   Shares, but I've sold Vanguard ETFs as I don't want to invest in gambling, weapons, etc.

3. *What's the breakdown of your shares?*

   A200: 50.27%, GL1: 4.12%, PPK: 10.88%, WDS: 9.90%, YAL: 24.83%.

4. *How much do you invest and how often?*

   Usually $1000 monthly.

5. *What are your money goals?*

   Passive income so I can be comfortable during retirement.

6. *How much debt do you have?*

   Mortgage: $410k.

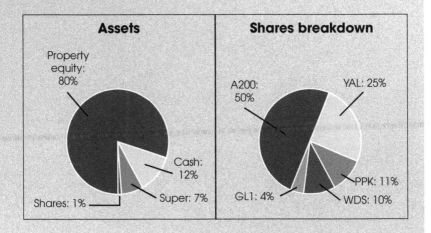

7. *What's your biggest financial challenge?*

   Understanding how to invest ethically on my own terms.

8. *What's your biggest money mistake?*

   Investing in dodgy stocks.

9. *How are you building a life you love through investing?*

   I'm working towards a potential early retirement or switching to part-time work in the next 10 to 15 years. At the moment, I am investing $300 per month into an employee share plan, at the end of the three-year plan, I will get one share for every two shares bought (provided I stay with the company for 3 years). Additional to this, I'm targeting investing $2000–$5000 per year in shares/ETFs to build my passive income. I have not yet invested this year as I'm facing the challenge of which shares/ETFs as I want to make sure these are ethical from my perspective/beliefs. I also salary sacrifice $2300 per year, I will be doubling in the future.

   Our property is on a big piece of land with a studio at the back, we plan to renovate / extend this studio and rent it out — this will be passive income. Once the studio is completed, we will look at other potential property investments.

Chapter 7

Let's talk super

A note about this chapter: It's important to check the ATO website for up-to-date information and requirements as the rules in relation to super change constantly.

If you have a super account, you're already an investor.

In Australia, super is a powerful—yet often underestimated—tool for building wealth. It's a compulsory way of saving for your retirement. For most people, retirement may feel like a lifetime away so it's easy to disengage, but if you're planning to not work forever, then it's essential that you have a handle on your super and the money in it. Although the money in your super can't be accessed until preservation age (which is currently 60), it still needs to be considered as part of your overall investing strategy.

The government mandates that your employer needs to contribute a percentage of your income into your super (as long as you meet all the criteria), but you can also contribute extra. This money is then invested into a diversified portfolio called MySuper by default, which comprises cash, bonds, property, shares and alternative investments (such as infrastructure, private equity).

Australia's super system is very complex, with a lot of regulations and rules — in fact, it's one of the most complex retirement funding systems in the world — so we're going to break down the essentials for you.

What is super?

Super is a tax structure that holds investments. Super is not an investment in itself, but the money inside your super is invested. Money is contributed to your super by your employer to fund your life once you retire. There are limits on when you can withdraw your money to spend it, but you can usually access your super when you change jobs or retire after the age of 60, or when you reach age 65. Between ages 60 and 65 you can access 10 per cent of your super each year via a transition to retirement pension, even if you don't meet the former criteria.

In most circumstances (there are a few exceptions), your employer must put contributions into your super account. This is referred to as the superannuation guarantee (SG). SG was introduced with a mandatory 3 per cent contribution rate in 1992 and it was designed to ensure that all workers in Australia would save for retirement.

As at 1 July 2023, the superannuation guarantee was 11 per cent per year, and it has been legislated to increase each year over the next few years until it reaches 12 per cent per year.

Your employer must pay a minimum amount—based on the current SG rate and your ordinary earnings—into your super account. Super is generally not paid on overtime hours.

You can also contribute extra money to your super account yourself, and the government incentivises this by offering tax benefits, which we'll address in this chapter.

How to choose a super fund

Chances are you already have a super fund. However, if you're thinking of switching funds, it's a good idea to ensure your super is in a high-performing, low-fee fund. This can have a huge impact on the quality of your retirement. Most people sign up to the fund chosen by their employer, but you can choose to switch to another fund if you wish, so it's worth shopping around to check you're getting a good deal.

There are four main things you should consider when comparing super funds:

1. Fees

2. Investment options

3. Investment performance

4. Insurance within super.

1. Fees

Fees ... argh, *that* word. As your super fund is an investment service, you have to pay super fund fees for investing and managing your money.

All super funds charge fees — these may include an administration fee and an investment fee. They may be displayed as a dollar amount, as a percentage figure or as both. Administration fees are usually deducted monthly and after actions such as switching to a different investment portfolio. Investment fees are usually reflected in the unit price, which means that fees are taken from the total pool of super assets before the price of each unit is calculated.

If you're really interested in how it works, here's a breakdown (but don't stress too much about how it's calculated).

If the fund's assets (after all expenses and liabilities except investment fees) are worth $100 million and there are 10 million units, the unit price before fees might be $10.00. If investment fees of $1 million are deducted, the assets would reduce to $99 million. The new unit price would be calculated as $99 million / 10 million units = $9.90. The decrease from $10.00 to $9.90 reflects the impact of investment fees.

You'll want to aim for lower fees, unless your fund is providing you with something that justifies the higher fees, such as an ethical investment option. As a general rule, you should aim to keep your *total* super fees under 1 per cent per annum, but be sure to work out what your total super fees are. It's easy to miss the administration fees when they're displayed as a separate dollar amount.

As a guide, Canstar found that the super funds on their database charge on average between 0.91 per cent and 1.21 per cent each year in fees.

How much do fees actually matter?

A 1-per-cent difference in fees may not seem like a huge amount, but over time and as your super balance grows, these can really add up. Here's an example.

Alex is 30 years old and earns $80 000 a year, excluding super. Their super balance is currently $50 000 and they are aiming to retire at 60. Alex has a choice of two super funds.

	Annual fees	Total return at 60	Fees paid
Super fund A	1 per cent	$417 422	$85 893
Super fund B	2 per cent	$354 141	$149 174

Assuming 7 per cent annual rate of return and 11 per cent annual employer contribution, that's a difference of $63 281 at retirement.

2. Investment options

Your super fund is basically a tax-efficient vehicle that holds your investments. This means that most super funds have a range of different investment options for you to choose from.

Unless you've chosen an option yourself, your money is likely invested into something called the MySuper option. This is usually made up of 70–80 per cent growth investments (shares and property) and 20–30 per cent defensive investments (bonds and cash).

You can choose to change your investment mix to something other than the default option. It's worth noting that super-fund options aren't standardised and 'balanced': one fund may hold a very different percentage of defensive assets than another balanced fund. So when comparing funds, make sure to compare apples with apples, and not apples with oranges.

You should be able to pick from investment options based on risk—for example:

- cash

- conservative

- balanced

- growth

- high growth.

Some funds also offer ethical options.

Your age and predicted retirement age will largely influence which option you pick and the level of risk you take on. As you won't be able to access your super until you retire or reach preservation age, you might have 10–40 years before you can withdraw money from super, depending on your current age.

Just like investing outside of your super, knowing your risk tolerance is important. Someone closer to retirement may want to hold more bonds or cash (defensive assets), whereas someone in their 20s may be happy to hold a larger percentage of shares or riskier assets because they have a longer time horizon available to ride out any volatility.

Before changing your super investments or superfund, you should make sure you've done your research. If you chop and change there can be additional fees payable (called buy-sell spreads), and there may also be tax implications. Not to mention the potential loss of insurance (more on this below). Do your research, find a good fund, and stick with it (unless they really start doing a bad job).

Not sure which investment option is right for you? Your super fund most likely offers free advice to help you choose.

3. Investment performance

The next thing to consider when choosing a super fund is its performance. Compare your super fund's investment performance over a 5-year period, or longer (remember, you're investing for the long term).

Table 7.1 (overleaf) presents the top-performing super funds as ranked by SuperRatings over the last 1, 3, and 5 years in the Growth category (77–90 per cent growth assets). You'll notice there's no clear winner across all periods. Attempting to predict which super fund will outperform in the future is as challenging as picking individual stocks to beat the market. The takeaway? Choose a super fund that's currently performing well, but make sure to check how they are performing each year. If they start underperforming, it might be time to consider making a change.

If you want to check how your super fund is comparing, you can use the super heatmaps created by the Australian Prudential Regulation Authority (APRA). The aim of these heatmaps is to increase the transparency around super product offerings and their performance. The heatmaps highlight which funds are performing, which have poor performance and which have significantly poor performance.

But remember that not all super funds are created equal (you've heard that before, haven't you?). You can start by comparing a balanced fund to another balanced fund, but not all balanced funds have the same allocation to growth and defensive assets. For example, some balanced funds have 50 per cent growth assets and 50 per cent defensive assets, while others have 75 per cent growth assets and 25 per cent defensive assets.

Table 7.1: the top 5 super funds in the growth category

Top 5 funds over each time period (based on annual return)	1 year	3 years	5 years
1	Vanguard Super SaveSmart - High Growth	Australian Retirement Trust - Super Savings - Growth	Brighter Super Optimiser Accumulation - Multi-Manager High Growth Fund
2	Brighter Super Optimiser Accumulation - Multi-Manager High Growth Fund	Qantas Super - Aggressive	Australian Retirement Trust - Super Savings - Growth
3	OnePath OA Frontier - OnePath High Growth Index	HESTA - High Growth	HESTA - High Growth
4	Prime Super - Managed Growth	First Super - Growth	Vision Super - Growth
5	ESSSuper Accumulation - Growth	Australian Food Super - Growth	Cbus Super - High Growth

* Past performance is not a reliable indicator of future returns. Returns are net of investment fees. Returns are net of investment fees, but before administration fees charged by the super fund. Before making any changes, you should read the Product Disclosure Statement & Target Market Determination to learn more about the product you're interested in, including fees and risks. Some of these super funds may be restricted to certain industries. Returns as at 31 December 2023.

Source: Top 10 Super Funds, Growth category (77–90% growth assets), SuperRatings, as at 29 February 2024.

The ATO MySuper comparison tool is a great way to compare other MySuper products. You'll find another useful tool on Industry Super Australia's website. This tool is powered by SuperRatings (a leading research agency) and it allows you to compare all major funds. It provides tailored comparisons for each person's circumstance, taking into consideration fees, returns and insurance, among other things. It's important to remember that past performance is not indicative of future returns (you've definitely heard that before!), which means that just because a fund has performed well previously, this doesn't mean it will continue to do so in the future.

4. Insurance within super

Why do you need insurance? Think about what you do when you buy a new car. The first thing you do is purchase car insurance, right?

For the average car worth $20 000, $30 000 or maybe $40 000, this would cost about $1300 each year. So if we insure our cars, why don't we place more importance on insuring ourselves and our ability to earn an income?

Did you know that in Australia one in eight females will be diagnosed with breast cancer by the time they are 85? And one in six males will be diagnosed with prostate cancer by the time they are 85.

Most Australians are underinsured. This is because it can be seen as costly, there is an overwhelming number of product options and it can be confusing working out where to start.

There are three main types of insurance available that you can acquire within super or personally (outside super):

- *Life insurance* — paid as a lump-sum payment upon death. There's also the option of receiving a payment in the event of a terminal illness.

- *Total and permanent disability (TPD) insurance* — paid as a lump-sum payment. The requirements are that you must be fully disabled and unable to look after yourself or ever work again. This cover is cheaper, but has a higher threshold to claim.

  Note: There are different definitions of what it means to be totally and permanently disabled depending on the provider and type of job. The definitions generally include that you're unable to work in any job suited to your education, training or experience.

- *Income protection* — paid as a regular income to replace your salary. This cover generally insures up to 70 per cent of your income and usually includes a waiting and benefit period before you can access it. Waiting periods can be up to 2 years. The requirements are that you are not able to work or perform the main duties of your job due to an injury or illness at the end of your waiting period. If you buy an income protection policy outside of super, generally the insurance premiums are tax deductible.

Should you get insurances within super? For many people, insurance through your super can often be cheaper because it's bought in bulk for lots of people at once. But there's a big difference: if you use super for insurance, it means you'll have

> *less money saved up for when you retire because you're using some of it now. With non-super insurance, you pay from your pocket, so your super savings won't be touched. There's pros and cons with both options.*

There are also two types of insurance only available outside of super:

- *Trauma/critical illness insurance* — paid as a lump-sum payment that covers you for specific illnesses such as cancer, stroke and heart attack. There are also accident-only trauma policies, which are cheaper, but beware of taking these out as three out of four trauma claims are for medical reasons, not due to accident.

- *TPD insurance (own occupation definition)* — policies outside of super can offer this definition, which means you are considered totally and permanently disabled if you can no longer work in your specific profession. This cover is more expensive, but provides a higher level of cover that's generally easier to qualify for if you need to make a claim (and avoid needing to potentially retain in other roles/jobs you may be suited for).

TPD insurance: how to get the best of both worlds

Super-linked TPD policies offer a hybrid solution that allows you to hold part of the policy — the 'any occupation' part — inside super making use of the tax benefits. The 'own occupation' part is then held outside of super, ensuring that part of the cover meets the more specific definition of disability. You will want to engage a financial advisor if you're taking out one of these policies because they are complex to structure.

When should you start considering this type of insurance?

Here are some examples of when it's important to consider taking out or updating your insurance:

- when taking on financial responsibility, such as buying a home, getting married and starting a family

- in the event of an inheritance/a windfall

- after a big salary increase or job change

- as your family wealth goes up, in which case your insurance needs go down

- when you are young and healthy because it's easier to get insurance as there are fewer underwriting requirements

- when you open your first super account because you're likely to have default coverage that you may need to update for your specific needs.

> *Do you have the correct insurance? When signing up to a super fund, you may have a default level of cover. A single 23 year old in their first job, still living at home and madly saving enough for a deposit on their first home may not need to be paying for death cover (unless they want to leave a windfall for their parents).*

Before moving super funds, it's crucial to check what insurance you have and to ensure you can get appropriate insurance elsewhere before switching funds. New insurance cover may be more expensive or you may even be declined cover if your circumstances have changed, especially if a new health issue has arisen and you're deemed as too risky. They could apply loadings or exclusions to your new cover – meaning you will likely be better off by keeping your existing cover.

Super funds often come with a default level of cover. When comparing these you should consider:

- the premium rates (the cost of the insurance)

- the amount of cover

- any exclusions or definitions that might affect you.

It's worth seeing a financial advisor to sort out your insurance. Advisors often receive a commission from the insurance providers so there's no upfront cost to you. If you can afford to pay your advisor an upfront fee, it's worth discussing this with them as they may be able to turn off the commission, thereby reducing the cost of your insurance premiums.

Some financial advice businesses, such as Guideway Wealth, may be able to sort out your insurance free of charge by using commissions from a new home loan. So, if you need a new mortgage or to refinance a current mortgage, it might be a great time to get your insurance looked at too.

Adding more to your super

Okay, so now that you've picked a super fund and have your insurance organised, next let's look at how to top up your super contributions.

Regardless of your age and where you are on your investment journey, it's important to consider your super as part of your retirement investment strategy. For example, if you're closer to retirement and have money to spare, considering your super as a part of your strategy may be beneficial due to the tax advantages. If you're younger, you might be thinking, 'Retirement is so far away. Is it really worth adding extra money to my super fund?'

We'll let you decide for yourself with an example.

Table 7.2 demonstrates the impact of contributing $1825 extra each year (that's just $5 extra each day) to your super.

Table 7.2: the benefits of contributing $5 to your super every day

	Starting balance	Additional contributions	Balance after 35 years
Scenario A	$20k	$0	$562 662
Scenario B	$20k	$1825/year	$664 245

Using the AustralianSuper Super Projection Calculator. Assuming an income of $80 000/year, age 30 in 2024, high-growth portfolio, retiring in 35 years at 65.

Adding just $1825 per year ($5 a day) can earn you $101 583 more in your super fund over 35 years. This significant difference highlights how small, regular amounts can really add up over the longer term.

When you voluntarily put money into your super fund, you might qualify for an income-tax deduction, which means you could get some money back at tax time just for adding to your super. It's like a small 'thank you' from the tax office for thinking ahead and saving for your future! And here's the icing on the cake: these tax benefits really kick in when your personal tax rate is higher than the 15 per cent rate that applies to concessional super contributions (we will explain this shortly). So if you're in a higher tax bracket, putting money into your super could be a smart way to save on tax and boost your retirement savings at the same time. The income-tax deduction doesn't happen automatically though. You'll have to fill in a 'Notice of intent to claim' and add the deduction to your tax return. We recommend speaking to an accountant for help with claiming any deductions on voluntary super contributions.

Now, you may be thinking, why invest in my super to save for retirement when I can invest outside of super? Well, super provides you with tax benefits that you can't access by investing outside of super. The maximum tax rate on investment earnings within super is 15 per cent, and capital gains tax can be as low as 10 per cent within super if the asset is held for more than 12 months thanks to the 12-month CGT discount rule.

If you were to invest outside of your super through a broker, any dividend earnings would be taxed at your marginal tax rate (also referred to as your personal tax rate, this is the threshold you're taxed at based on a percentage of your income earnings), which could be as high as 45 per cent. Therefore, if your marginal tax rate is above 15 per cent it may be advantageous to consider investing through your super.

Okay, so now let's explore how to add money to your super fund.

As you've no doubt already realised, the finance industry likes complicated jargon, and the super industry is no different. 'Concessional contributions' and 'non-concessional contributions' are two super-related terms you'll want to understand. They describe the two main ways to contribute money to super.

Table 7.3 (overleaf) illustrates the difference between them.

Table 7.3: the differences between concessional and non-concessional super contributions

Contribution	Tax	2023–2024 Cap	2024–2025 Cap*
Concessional (pre-tax) *For example, employer contribution, salary sacrifice, personal contributions with tax deduction.*	15% on entry into super	$27500 per year	$30000 per year
Non-concessional (after tax) *For example, after-tax spousal contribution and personal contribution.*	Not taxed on entry into super	$110000 per year *(bring forward $330 000 over 3 years)*	$120000 per year *(bring forward $360000 over 3 years)*

*Legislated at time of writing but subject to change

Super contribution caps can change – they are indexed, and the Government does love to make changes to them! So before making any super contribution, contact your super fund and they'll help make sure you stay within the caps free of charge. You can also check the Australian Tax Office (ATO) portal through your myGov login. If you go outside the caps, you can get hit with penalties from the ATO.

Let's break down what each means and how you can use it to contribute to your super.

Concessional contributions (pre-tax)

One of the primary reasons for adding extra into your super fund is for the tax benefits.

Concessional contributions are taxed at a (concessional) rate of 15 per cent *inside* a super fund. They're also called pre-tax contributions because they're taken from your pay before you've paid tax on them. This concessional rate is beneficial because it is generally less than your marginal tax rate (which can be as high as 45 per cent).

Concessional contributions include:

- *personal contributions made from your after-tax income.* You are eligible to claim these as an income tax deduction. Even though you make these contributions from your net income (that is, your income after tax has been deducted), by claiming them as a deduction, you effectively convert them into concessional (pre-tax) contributions

- *employer contributions* such as:

    - employer superannuation guarantee contributions (the compulsory amount your employer pays)

    - any salary sacrifice (also called salary package) contributions: an arrangement with your employer to add a portion of your pre-tax salary to your super, providing immediate tax benefits.

Think of salary sacrificing as sacrificing a part of your salary so that it's invested plus you get a tax break.

Salary sacrificing is when you arrange to have some of your salary paid into your super account instead of directly to you. The salary sacrificed (or packaged) amount is not assessable income for tax purposes. This means your taxable income is reduced and these contributions are taxed in your super fund at the concessional rate of 15 per cent.

If you earn more than $45000 per year, then making extra concessions is tax effective, but there is a limit to how much you can contribute. The total allowable concessional contribution (the one that gets the dreamy 15 per cent tax rate) is currently $27500 per financial year and is legislated to increase to $30000 from 1 July 2024.

This amount also includes your employer contributions, as well as any extra concessional contributions you make. This is something to be cognisant of if you're a high-income earner because you might reach that threshold quickly due to the 11 per cent your employer contributes. You can only claim a tax deduction on the voluntary concessional contributions you make.

Catch-up concessional contributions

You may be eligible to contribute more using something called 'catch-up concessional contributions' if you haven't reached your concessional contribution caps in previous years. To take advantage of this, your total super balance must be below $500000 on 30 June of the previous financial year. Catch-up concessional contributions enable you to 'carry forward' any unused concessional contributions from the previous 5 years.

Catch-up concessional contributions can be a good idea for those with a bigger influx of money one year, resulting in a higher tax bill (concessional contributions lower your taxable income). Examples could include after selling a property, receiving a redundancy payout or selling shares. You can login to the ATO Portal through myGov and it'll tell you how much you can contribute under this rule. Figure 7.1 explains how concessional contributions work.

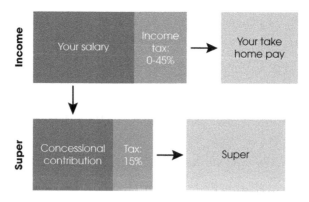

Figure 7.1: how (pre-tax) concessional contributions work

Non-concessional contributions (after-tax)

Non-concessional contributions are also called 'after-tax contributions'. The benefit of non-concessional contributions is that you don't have to pay tax when you put your money into your super because you have already paid tax on your money and are using your after-tax money to contribute to your super. Your earnings within super will be taxed at a maximum rate of 15 per cent, which is still a huge benefit in comparison to investing outside of your super.

Non-concessional contributions include:

- contributions you or your employer make from your after-tax income that you don't claim a tax deduction on

- contributions your spouse makes to your super (with some exceptions).

Table 7.4 shows the caps and limits for 2024/25 financial year.

Table 7.4: non-concessional super contribution caps for 2024/25

Total Super balance at 30 June 2024*	Non-concessional contribution cap for 2024/25
$1.9m+	$0
$1.78m < $1.9m	$120000
$1.66m < $1.78m	$240000^
< $1.66m	$360000^

* At the time of writing this is projected for the 2024/25 FY (but it may be changed by the time the book gets published, so make sure you double check with your superfund before making a non-concessional contribution).
^ If you use the bring-forward rule (more on this overleaf).
Source: © Commonwealth of Australia.

The bring-forward rule

There's also something called the 'bring-forward rule' for non-concessional contributions. This is a shorter term period than the concessional contributions that we spoke about previously (5 years), and it allows you to bring forward your non-concessional contribution caps for the next 2 years if your total super balance is below a certain amount. This means you can contribute up to $360 000 in the 2024/25 financial year depending on your total super balance on 30 June 2024. The bring-forward rule is a popular strategy for those who want to move a larger sum of money into their super — for example, from selling an investment property or receiving an inheritance. See figure 7.2 for details on how non-concessional (after-tax) contributions work.

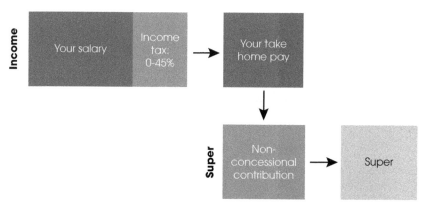

Figure 7.2: how non-concessional (after-tax) contributions work

It's important to remember that limits apply to both types of contributions: concessional (pre-tax) contributions and non-concessional (after-tax) contributions. These limits depend on your age, previous contributions and the balance of your super account. Be sure to speak to an accountant and/or financial advisor for advice on your situation.

How to make the most of your super

But wait ... there's even more good news about super. There are a couple of legit ways you might be able to get additional benefits from your super.

Low-income super tax offset

If you earn $37000 per annum or less (at the time of writing), up to $500 is paid back into your super account courtesy of the low-income super tax offset (LISTO). The ATO works this out for you, and if you're eligible they'll pay the money into your super account. You don't need to do anything.

Government co-contributions

If you earn less than $58445 per annum (at the time of writing), the government may match your after-tax super contributions with a co-contribution of up to $500. If you qualify, the ATO will deposit the co-contribution directly into your super fund.

Spouse super contributions

If you want to contribute to your spouse's or de facto partner's super account, you can do this in two different ways.

One option is to make an after-tax contribution directly into their super account, treating it as a non-concessional contribution. This may entitle you to a tax offset.

Contribution splitting

Alternatively, you can transfer a portion of your super contributions to your spouse's account. There are a few hoops to jump through with this option, therefore, it can be difficult to achieve. However, it may be worth it for couples wanting to support one another in retirement, especially for parents who forgo paid work to stay home with the kids and therefore miss out on super payments.

First home super saver scheme (FHSS scheme)

The FHSS Scheme is a way to save for your home deposit inside your super fund. It is designed to help boost savings for a first home by allowing people to build their deposit inside their super fund and take advantage of the lower tax rates.

You are able to make voluntary contributions and, subject to eligibility requirements, have these contributions and their associated earnings released to purchase your first home.

Currently, you can contribute $50 000 per person, but you can only contribute up to $15 000 per financial year (not part of your employer's SG) into your super towards the scheme. This means that you'll need to start planning well ahead of buying a home to make the most of the scheme.

Once you withdraw your deposit, you'll need to sign a contract to purchase or construct a home within 12 months; otherwise you may have to pay an additional tax potentially costing you more than if you had not done the FHSS Scheme in the first place.

Contributions you make under the FHSS Scheme count towards your concessional or non-concessional contribution limits each year. Speak to a financial adviser, accountant or your superfund to find out whether you will be better off making FHSS Scheme contributions as concessional or non-concessional contributions.

Check out figure 7.3 if the FHSS Scheme is something that interests you.

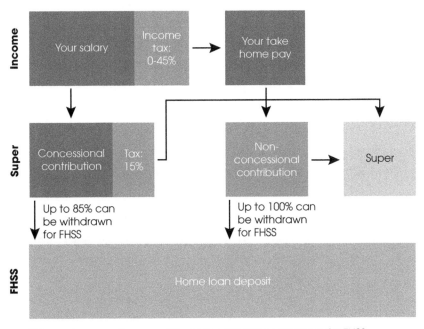

*Compulsory employer contributions cannot be withdrawn for FHSS

Figure 7.3: how the FHSS Scheme works

How we think about our super

Ana: I've always considered super 'my money', whereas I'd hear others say, 'I won't even think about my super since I can't access it for ages'. As someone who's always calculated my net worth, super has always been something I actively tracked.

For the longest time, I was unsure if I would stay in Australia (as a Canadian citizen) so I didn't want to lock my money away into super. However, when I finally decided to buy a house with my partner, I elected to salary sacrifice to access the FHSS Scheme. This was the only time I actively contributed to my super.

That being said, I previously invested in my Canadian equivalent of a retirement fund many years ago and feel comfortable with the amount of money I will eventually retire with.

Tash: For years, super didn't really excite me. Waiting for the age of 65 to come around felt like forever away. I started investing at 18 and I liked the idea of having immediate access to my money if I changed my mind or needed it for something. As I've gotten further along my journey, I now realise how much of a huge impact the tax benefits from investing inside super can have. While I still want to have most of my investments outside of super at this stage of my life, I will start to make more use of concessional contributions to reduce my tax liability. With the current average female life expectancy in Australia sitting at 85.3 at the time of writing, my super will still be needed to fund about 25 years of my life after retirement.

When can you access your super?

Now that you understand the financial benefits of investing inside your super and how to get money in there, let's talk about how to get your money back out.

There are a few circumstances under which you can access your super:

- when you turn 65, even if you haven't retired

- when you reach preservation age of 60 and retire or change employers

- if you reach age 60 but are still working you might be able to access up to 10 per cent of your super each year using the transition to retirement (TTR) scheme — if your super fund offers it as an option

- when you satisfy an early access requirement such as:

  - on medical, compassionate or hardship grounds

  - the FHSS Scheme

  - permanent incapacity: if you're deemed to be unable to work again in a job you were qualified for (by education, training or experience)

  - if you're a temporary resident leaving Australia.

Now to us, 'preservation' reminds us of jam or things preserved in jars. But in the context of super, it's the age at which you can ordinarily access your super.

Once you meet the conditions to access your super, you're entitled to access it tax free. You can choose to withdraw it, or move it into something called an account-based pension (which gives you a regular income stream when you retire using the money from your super). An account-based pension can be a great option as any investment returns are tax free.

How much super do you need?

The Association of Superannuation Funds of Australia (ASFA) releases regular retirement standards that include how much super you'd need for retirement and what your retirement budget would look like based on your super balance. Table 7.5 sets this out, while table 7.6 summarises three retirement lifestyles.

Table 7.5: super balances required at retirement

Savings required	Modest		Comfortable	
	Single	Couple	Single	Couple
	$100000	$100000	$595000	$690000

Source: © Copyright 2024 ASFA

Now, an important thing to note here is that the retirement standards and figures are based on someone owning their home outright. If you don't plan on having a fully paid-off property, need to plan for unexpected events such as divorce or want to travel more than every 7 years, then you will need to plan for more.

Table 7.6: the definition of comfortable and modest retirement lifestyle expectations based on super balance

	Comfortable lifestyle	Modest lifestyle	Age pension
Health	Top level private health insurance, doctor/specialist visits, pharmacy needs	Basic private health insurance, limited gap payments	No private health insurance
Internet	Fast reliable internet/telco subscription, computer/android mobile /streaming services	Basic mobile, modest internet data allowance	Very basic mobile and limited internet connectivity
Car	Own a reasonable car, car insurance and maintenance / upkeep	Owning a cheaper, older, more basic car	Limited budget to own, maintain or repair a car
Leisure	Regular leisure activities including club membership, cinema visits, exhibitions, dance/ yoga classes	Infrequent leisure activities, occasional trip to the cinema	Rare trips to the cinema
Home	Home repairs, updates and maintenance to kitchen and bathroom appliances over 20 years	Limited budget for home repairs, household appliances	Struggle to pay for repairs, such as leaky roofs or major plumbing problem

(continued)

Table 7.6: the definition of comfortable and modest retirement lifestyle expectations based on super balance (*cont'd*)

	Comfortable lifestyle	Modest lifestyle	Age pension
Haircuts	Regular professional haircuts	Budget haircuts	Less frequent haircuts, or self-haircuts
Heating/cooling	Confidence to use air-conditioning in the home, afford all utilities	Need to keep a close watch on all utility costs and make sacrifices	Limited budget for home heating in winter
Dining out	Occasional restaurant meals, home-delivery meals, take-away coffee	Limited meals out at inexpensive restaurants, infrequent home-delivery or takeaway	Only local club special meals or inexpensive takeaway
Clothing	Replace worn-out clothing and footwear items, modest wardrobe updates	Limited budget to replace or update worn items	Very basic clothing and footwear budget
Travel	Annual domestic trip to visit family, one overseas trip every seven years	Annual domestic trip or a few short breaks	Occasional short break or day trip in your own city

Source: © Copyright 2024 ASFA

Other super considerations

Although super is undoubtedly a fantastic way to save for retirement, there are some legislative risks worth knowing about. Due to super being regulated by the government, the rules can change at any time. In fact, the preservation age has previously been lifted from 55 to 60, and there's always the chance that it might be adjusted again. Recently, the government introduced a tax on super balances over $3 million, which is to be implemented in July 2025.

To access your personal super information, such as your contributions, cap contribution limits and any thresholds, you can do so through your myGov account.

How to incorporate your super to build a life you love

Depending on where you are on your financial journey, super may be part of your strategy to build an amazing life.

You may want to invest outside of your super so you can access your money earlier. This would enable you to receive dividends in the form of income and to sell shares when needed. It can give you the opportunity to start a business or take a sabbatical. Having money easily accessible can be beneficial. As such, investing outside of your super does provide you with more flexibility.

However, your circumstances may be that you're close to retirement. Perhaps your strategy is to take advantage of tax savings and increase your contributions for a very comfortable retirement where you can travel the world carefree. In this case, investing through your super may be more beneficial.

In a different scenario, you may want to save for your first home through the FHSS Scheme, in which case you'd want to salary sacrifice (concessional contributions) into your super to receive a tax benefit as you save for your downpayment.

Or maybe you just want to reduce your work to part-time to stay at home and look after your kids and your partner might co-contribute through a spousal contribution to ensure you have enough money for your retirement.

Like all things in life, your strategy when it comes to super may change, depending on your age and what assets you acquire. Regardless of your goals, it is important to consider super for your retirement.

Make a start

Let's talk super

- Use the *Moneysmart* compound interest and super calculators to see how much switching funds could save you in fees, what your balance will be at retirement and the impact adding extra money could have on your total super balance.

- Check your super fund to see what your money is invested in: a high-growth diversified fund, all cash, all shares or a balanced option?

- Check whether you have adequate insurance within your super and what you're covered for.

- Calculate whether you can invest in your super through salary sacrifice or after-tax contributions and by how much this could reduce your tax liability.

- If you're planning on stopping work early (prior to your preservation age) to retire, make sure you have enough invested for a comfortable retirement.

- Listen to some of the 'super' episodes on the *Get Rich Slow Club* podcast.

Case Study

Alicia, 26

1. *Annual income:* 96k

2. *Source of income:* Full-time teacher.

3. *What investing platform do you use?*

   I use Pearler for my investing (as well as my super platform). I did use Spaceship but because of the fees and how little I had invested I sold those and put them into Micro through Pearler.

4. *What do you currently invest in?*

   95% cash, 5% ETFs.

5. *What's the breakdown of your shares?*

   34% Micro, 47% QUAL, 13% REIT, 6% VESG.

6. *How much do you invest and how often?*

   $100/fortnight.

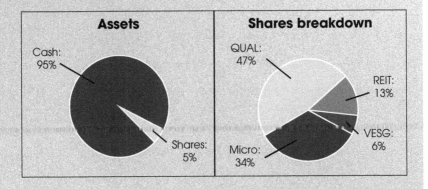

7. *What are your money goals?*

Set myself up financially. At the moment, investing isn't a priority as I am saving for a deposit for my first property.

8. *What's your biggest financial challenge?*

The cost of a mortgage for a cheaper property in my area on a single wage.

9. *What's your investing strategy?*

At the beginning it was to invest an initial amount in ETFs and let the money sit for a small amount of time so I could become familiar with the stock market and seeing the small dips and not panicking. Now as I'm saving for a deposit I am just investing in micro and then will resume with ETFs.

10. *What's your biggest money mistake?*

Not saving when I first moved out of home and interstate with my first teaching gig. I spent all my money in the first year and have no idea where it went. I am now more intentional with my purchases and pay more attention to what I am spending it on.

11. *Any advice for new investors?*

For anyone wanting to invest—simply just start! It can be scary to start with but just investing a little bit and watching your balance change over a period of time can allow you to become comfortable with watching your money go up and down.

12. *How are you building a life you love through investing?*

At this stage in my life I am simply just exploring the world of investing. I didn't have any education about it while growing up and am still learning every day. I love to travel and explore new places, so by investing I hope that this will allow for me to retire early/take more time off of work so that I can travel as much as possible. I hope that by the age of 30 I have more of an idea of what I am doing and have carved out a plan as to what I will be doing to set myself up financially.

Chapter 8

You've invested— now what?

Fantastic ... you've invested. Congratulations!

You're in the market and you're looking forward to compounding doing its thing. But ... now what?

Of course, investing is a long-term commitment, but there's a bunch of other things to consider while investing, such as the administrative work of tracking and selling shares, how to look at the performance and ultimately how to live the life you love thanks to your investments.

Investing administration

You're either one of those people who dreads admin or who loves getting out the spreadsheets and having a grasp of all things administrative.

For those who hate any type of paperwork (digital or not), there's unfortunately a bit of admin work you need to do when investing. But if you're on top of it, it will make your life so much easier come tax time.

And it's not too much work. We promise.

What's CHESS-Sponsored, again?

If you're invested in a Clearing House Electronic Subregister System (CHESS)-Sponsored product you have direct ownership of your shares.

As we saw, in Australia CHESS is the system used to keep track of the ownership of shares. It's an electronic record-keeping system that ensures everything is properly recorded, tracked and efficient.

You already know that along with your CHESS-Sponsored shares you receive a unique holder identification number (HIN), which is a special identification number for your shares. It's kind of like a bank account number. This helps with the accounting and tracking of your shares.

All of this tracking is done through share registries, which are something you need to know about.

Share registries

A share registry is an organisation whose role it is to maintain the records of shareholders of publicly listed companies. Registries have the following responsibilities:

- They record changes in ownership of shares.

- They issue statements (regarding buying and selling of shares).

- They manage dividend payments, bonuses and rights issues.

When you purchase a CHESS-Sponsored ETF or share, you will need to create an account with a share registry so you can instruct them on what to do with your dividends, as well as any other actions taken by shareholders. It may take up to 2 weeks for an initial investment to be registered with the share registry.

Unfortunately, brokers do not manage this part for you.

There are three main registry companies in Australia: Computershare, Link Markets Services and BoardRoom.

How to register with a share registry

Once you purchase an ETF through a broker, you will receive a letter in the mail instructing you to visit the share registry website to create an account. You need to do this. Don't ignore or neglect the letter because it's really important for your security and to instruct the registry on how to treat your dividends (where to pay them, or if you want to set up a dividend reinvestment plan), among other things.

The reason it's important to register with the share registry is that for CHESS-Sponsored brokers, this is the official record-keeping method for shares and ETFs.

If something were to happen to the broker, you'd still have access to your investments through the registry and you could transfer them to another broker if needed.

Once you log on to the share registry, you'll need to enter your bank details and tax file number (TFN). This is so you can instruct the registry on how to pay your dividends (you can receive the income as a payment or have it reinvested).

Remember that the share registry is the official record keeper, so it's important that your information is up to date.

Dividend reinvestment plans

A dividend reinvestment plan (DRP) allows shareholders to reinvest all, or part, of their dividends into additional shares rather than receiving them as cash. Not all shares and ETFs offer this, so it's good to check.

There are a few things to consider when deciding whether or not a DRP suits your needs (vs receiving dividends as cash). Some of the pros of DRPs are:

- *compounding effect*. Reinvesting dividends is a great way to help your investments compound and grow through the purchase of more shares.

- *no brokerage fees*. Reinvested shares allow you to get extra shares without the brokerage fees. If you receive a $100 dividend in cash, paying the $5.50 brokerage fee to reinvest it yourself probably isn't worth it, whereas it's free if the dividend is reinvested through a DRP.

- *dollar-cost averaging.* DRPs will invest in a regular cadence as you receive your dividends (usually biannually).

- *potential discount.* Some companies offer discounts when DRPs are used to acquire new units of shares.

- *simplified investment process.* Automating your investments and using a DRP is the ultimate 'set and forget strategy'.

Some of the cons of DRPs are:

- *you still pay tax.* It doesn't matter if you get dividends paid in cash or through the DRP, you still need to pay tax on them. If you receive franking credits, you'll also need to claim these on your tax return.

- *no income stream.* Receiving an income is key when transitioning from living off employment income to living off investment income. As mentioned above, tax still needs to be paid, so if you're using a DRP, you won't be receiving your dividend as a cash payment, and you'll need to find cash to pay the tax from elsewhere.

- *changing strategy.* If you change your investing strategy and no longer want to invest in the particular share you've set a DRP for, you usually need to stop your DRP in order to use your dividends to invest in another share or ETF.

- *paperwork.* The paperwork can be more complex when selling shares because you have to ensure that the correct purchase price is calculated when CGT is applied.

- *unbalanced portfolio.* If you have a DRP set up for a share or ETF that takes up the biggest percentage of your portfolio, the DRP will buy more shares, which may result in an unbalanced portfolio. If your dividend is less than the cost to buy one share, then the registry will hold onto it for you until there is enough to buy a whole share.

How to set up a DRP

Setting up a DRP is pretty easy. All you need to do is fill out a DRP instruction form via the share registry portal. Then, once you've accumulated enough dividends that they can be reinvested as a whole unit, they will be reinvested for you.

The alternative to using a DRP is waiting until your dividends hit your bank account and then using the money to purchase more shares. Both options help with the compounding of your investment.

ASX CHESS statement portal

The Australian Securities Exchange (ASX) makes it possible to receive electronic notifications about your investments as opposed to printed letters. There are two main ways to do this.

You can either log on to the ASX CHESS statement portal on their website and access your statements there. Or, if your broker provides this option for you, you can turn it on via the broker's platform, which will provide you access.

This has reduced a lot of physical paperwork and mail that investors used to receive from the share registry about their investments.

ASX CHESS holding statements

CHESS statements are similar to bank statements in that they are a record of activity when it comes to your investments. On your statement, you can see the transactions and balance of your HIN (which is essentially your investing account) buying and selling history.

On your CHESS statement, you will also be able to see the number of units of a share. This can be helpful when you need to do accounting and taxes in the future.

What if I didn't invest in a CHESS-Sponsored product?

There are a few investment products that aren't CHESS-Sponsored. Some of them are investments bought through a custodial or micro-investing platform. Shares that are based in another country (also referred to as 'domiciled') also don't use CHESS for their tracking.

If this is the case for you, then you will have to rely on your broker for information regarding your investment, including transactions, dividends and tax statements.

Taxes

Each year you'll have to do your taxes. This will include claiming any dividends you've received or any shares you may have sold that triggered a capital gains tax (CGT).

The way you get taxed on shares depends on a few factors, including whether you're a resident or non-resident for tax purposes, how long you've held the shares, and whether you received any dividends or capital gains from the shares.

The general rules are as follows.

- *Dividend income* — if you receive dividends from your shares, they will generally be subject to tax. This is included in your overall taxable income based on your marginal tax rate. Franking credits also need to be considered here. We will discuss them later in the chapter as they work a bit differently.

- *Capital gains tax (CGT)* — if you sell your shares for more than you paid for them, you may need to pay CGT on the gains. If you've held the shares for more than 12 months, you may be eligible for a 50 per cent discount on the CGT you owe.

If you're a non-resident, you may be subject to non-resident withholding tax on any capital gains you make.

The ATO will usually automatically fill out your dividend information on your tax return under the 'Managed fund distributions' category when you do your taxes electronically. However, it is your responsibility to ensure that the information is accurate.

Taxation law can be complex, depending on your circumstances. The information here is just a general overview. It's always a good idea to seek professional advice from a qualified tax accountant or financial advisor to ensure you're meeting your tax obligations and taking advantage of any tax benefits that may be available to you.

What are franking credits?

Franking credits are a fun bonus that comes with investing in shares of Australian companies. Essentially, they are your share of tax paid by a company on the profits from dividends. Franking credits are designed to prevent double taxation of company profits, and they're a tax credit that comes with your dividends.

Without franking credits, a company would pay tax on its profits and then shareholders would also pay tax on the dividends they receive from those profits.

Instead, with franking credits, a company pays corporate tax on its profits, and the remaining after-tax profits are distributed to shareholders in the form of dividends. These dividends have a rebate attached to them—which is the franking credit—that consists of the amount of tax that was already paid by the company. Figure 8.1 illustrates this process.

Figure 8.1: how franking credits work

Both the dividend and the franking credit must be claimed at tax time. You may receive franking credits that are either fully franked (30 per cent tax has been paid before the investor receives the dividend) or partly franked (30 per cent tax has already been paid on part of the dividend).

The interesting part about franking credits is that the benefits are dependent on your individual marginal tax rate. If your tax rate is higher than the company tax rate of 30 per cent, you may need to pay tax on top of the franking credit. Alternatively, if it's lower than the corporate tax rate, you may receive a refund or have your tax liability reduced. Franking credits are especially popular with retirees because they help them generate additional income when investing in Australian shares.

See table 8.1 for an example of how your tax bracket affects your franking credits.

Table 8.1: how your tax bracket affects your franking credits at tax time

	Investor A	Investor B	Investor C
Dividends paid	$1000	$1000	$1000
Franking credits	$428.57	$428.57	$428.57
Taxable income (dividends + franking credits)	$1428.57	$1428.57	$1428.57
Marginal tax rate	0%	30%	45%
Tax payable or refund	$428.57 refund	$0	$214.29 tax payable

Australia is one of the few countries that has a system like franking credits, which makes us quite unique.

What is a W-8BEN and when do you use it?

Did you invest in shares that are outside the Australian stock market? If so, you may need to fill out a W-8BEN form.

A W-8BEN is a form mandated by the Internal Revenue Services (IRS) in the United States. It is used to collect taxpayer information on individuals who are non-residents of the United States. Basically, the United States wants to know who is investing directly in US companies and to record their tax information.

When you invest in international shares, you might have to pay a withholding tax. This tax — typically around 30 per cent — is taken out of any dividends you earn from your investments. But there's good news: you can potentially access a reduced withholding tax rate, down to 15 per cent, when you submit a W-8BEN form.

There are two situations where Australian investors might need to submit this form for their US equities.

The first is if you're trading US-domiciled Australian stocks (such as VTS or VEU, which are on the ASX). You can file the W-8BEN via the responsible share registry.

The second situation is if you're trading US stocks such as AAPL or GOOGL, which are on the NASDAQ. Some brokerages automatically fill and file this form for you when you register for a US trading account.

If this sounds too complicated, you can also buy Australian domiciled ETFs that have international exposure, such as VGS, VISM and VGE.

Tracking your investments

Once you've started investing, it's a good idea to track your investments. Brokers may not give you a complete picture of your investing journey so it's a good idea to track your investments elsewhere. This can make it easier for tax planning and also when you're ready to sell your shares.

The most important things to track are:

- the price you bought and sold your shares at

- any dividends you received (whether you got cash or used a DRP).

You can use platforms such as Sharesight, Navexa or even Google Sheets to help you track all of your transactions in one place.

You can also track your total returns, which include capital gains, dividends and even currency gains. Take a look at table 8.2.

Table 8.2: an example of how to track investments considering capital gains, dividends and currency gain, using VEU as an example from 10th July 2019 to 22nd April 2024

Portfolio Assets	Capital Gains	Dividends	Currency Gains	Total Returns
VEU.NYSE	1.94% p.a	3.2% p.a	2.24% p.a	7.44% p.a

For example, if the share price is down, you may still be in the green overall because of your dividends. This is something that many new investors forget to consider as the share price is only one aspect of the total returns on your investments. Currency can also have a big impact, so keep this in mind when investing in overseas companies.

You can download tax reports directly from the share registry at tax time. If you're still feeling overwhelmed, don't hesitate to reach out to an accountant for help.

How to sell shares

Selling shares should be as easy as purchasing shares through your broker. Similarly to purchasing, you are able to choose to sell via a limit order or a market order and to decide how many you should sell.

When you sell shares, you will need to pay a brokerage fee for the transaction, and it will take about 2 business days to process and for you to receive the funds on your account.

If you hold shares indirectly through a managed fund, you can sell units of the fund. There may be withdrawal costs associated with this (known as the sell spread).

Make sure to keep a copy of all your transactions so that it's easier to do your accounting come tax time.

It may be worth speaking to a registered tax agent before selling shares to discuss any CGT implications (or you can calculate this yourself) so you aren't surprised come tax time.

Considerations when selling shares

There's a bit to consider when selling shares, as selling can impact your goals, strategy and taxable income. Before selling, it may be worth running through the points discussed below to ensure you've taken into account everything you need to know beforehand.

Goals

One of the most important things to consider is how selling shares aligns with your goals, especially long-term ones. Is the reason you're selling aligned with why you bought the shares in the first place? Have you set a goal that aligns with the selling of your investments? Or has your goal changed and therefore the shares no longer align with your goal?

Your investment strategy

How will selling your shares align with your investment strategy? Will you need to rebalance your portfolio? Will selling the shares change your risk tolerance? Has the price of the shares changed and therefore made you consider how they are aligned with your overall strategy? Knowing your investment strategy and how it may be impacted by selling can keep you on course for the long term.

Timing

Is this the right time for you to sell? Once you sell your shares, the returns are crystallised. If you are nervous seeing the ups and downs of the share market, consider whether the investment aligns with your values. Why did you originally buy the shares and when were you planning to sell them? Is now the right time for you or are external factors impacting how you feel about selling your shares?

Tax implications

There's no way around tax. When you sell shares, there will always be tax implications to consider such as whether you have held your shares for longer than 12 months. Did you make a profit or a loss? How will this impact your marginal tax rate? Are you a non-resident?

Difficult tax lessons

 Ana: When my partner and I were purchasing our first family home, I sold some shares to help with the downpayment. The week we purchased our home we found out we were pregnant. I then applied for paid parental leave and the child-care subsidy and realised that I was ineligible for them that year due to having sold shares and being over the income threshold. Although the rules have changed since then, it was a hard lesson to learn. I wish I had done some tax planning prior to selling my shares as the loss of PPL and CCS impacted our financial family planning.

Make a start

You've invested, now what?

- Sign up to the share registry once you receive a letter from them. Make sure to check and add all your information including what you want to do with your dividends.

(continued)

- Sign up to a tracking platform such as Sharesight or Navexa so you can see your returns on dividends, capital growth and currency to have a holistic understanding of your investments.

- If you hold any US domicile shares, be sure to fill out a W-8BEN form via your registry, or check that your broker has done so.

- At tax time, make sure to have all the necessary documentation regarding your dividends, franking credits and any shares you may have sold.

- Reach out to a tax accountant who can help you with tax planning, especially when you are considering selling shares, to work out how that may impact your marginal tax rate and any subsidies you may have access to.

Case Study

Bianca, 23

1. *Annual income:* $67 500

2. *What do you currently invest in?* 100% shares.

3. *What's the breakdown of your shares?*

   IMPQ, small amounts in others, now it's 100% DHHF.

4. *How much do you invest and how often?*

   $200 per week into DHHF, $50 per week into super.

5. *What are your money goals?*

   I want to build wealth, work towards financial independence and provide a future for my children.

6. *How much debt do you have?*

   $40k HECS; 270k home loan (shared with partner).

7. *What's your biggest financial challenge?*

   Continuing to save/invest while my partner is medically unable to work.

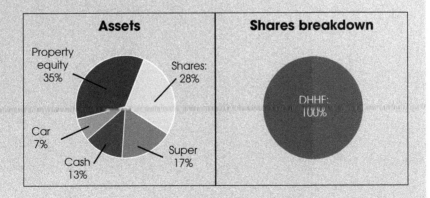

8. *What's your investing strategy?*

   Not following trends and not spending too long making investing decisions.

9. *What's your biggest money mistake?*

   Pulling out of stocks when they went down.

Chapter 9

How to live off your investments

We've all heard the saying 'time is money', but have you ever thought about what this really means? Time is a valuable resource because we don't have a lot of it. We all have a limited time on this earth — and even less time when we exchange our time for work.

If you work for 8 hours a day and sleep for 8 hours a night, you're effectively left with 8 hours a day of free time. Now if you take into consideration transportation, getting ready for the day, food prep and eating, family commitments and other obligations, that number of free hours starts to dwindle.

Time is finite so we really need to think about how we want to spend it. If we exchange our time for money for the rest of our life, we will effectively give up one of our most valuable resources.

So, how do you increase your free time?

One of the main ways to increase your free time is by having enough money to fund your lifestyle. Of course, we all wish we'd win the lottery or have a crazy business idea that we can sell for billions of dollars.

But the alternative is what this book is all about: using your investments to fund your lifestyle. The first step is to start investing.

Little by little you will grow your wealth and build a passive income stream. At first your dividend payment may be only 30 cents, but then it may grow to $30, then $300 and beyond.

The key to living off your investments is to invest early and often.

Okay, so you get the concept of making money to replace your work income. But how do you do this?

There are a few different ways to live off your investments. The first is to invest enough money so that your dividend income covers your expenses. To live off your dividends, the idea is that you don't touch your original investments (your capital) and continue to invest until your dividends increase to the point where they cover all your expenses or replace your salary.

Alternatively, you can invest until you think you have enough money to sell down your investments and live off the proceeds of the sales. This option will trigger CGT, which will be taxed at your marginal tax rate.

Or you can do a combination of the two: live off your dividends and sell down your investments. In practice, people will use dividends and then sell a portion of their investments to cover any gap between their dividend income and expenses. This way, investments are sold gradually over time and continue to receive dividends.

So, what's 'enough money' to live on?

How do you calculate how much money you need?

The Trinity Study reviewed more than 30 years of historic performances of different portfolios made up of shares (following the S&P 500) and bonds (long-term, high-grade corporations) to estimate when an investor would run out of money. The premise is that if you withdraw 4 per cent of your initial portfolio annually, you can sustain your lifestyle for at least 30 years. The withdrawal rate is the estimated percentage of money you're able to withdraw each year in retirement without running out of cash. This study also considers inflation in the calculation and is based on various percentage allocations including 100 per cent shares, 100 per cent bonds, and even a 50-per-cent share and 50-per-cent bond portfolio.

Those of you planning to retire for longer than 30 years may want to be more conservative with your calculations. Note that this study was undertaken using historical data — and as we know, past performance does not equal future performance.

So how do you calculate how much you need?

Your portfolio should be worth 25 times your annual expenses. Therefore, if your annual expenses are $40 000, you would need to invest about $1 million. Alternatively, if your expenses are $80 000 a year, you would need around $2 million in your portfolio. The theory is that you may be able to live off your investments indefinitely if you invested 25 times your annual expenses, adjusted for inflation.

To allow for inflation, let's say your investments are returning on average 7 per cent a year and you withdraw 4 per cent — that leaves you with 3 per cent for annual inflation and allows for your portfolio to continue to compound over time. Of course, this doesn't account for periods of high inflation or periods of market downturns, so it should only be used as a guide that you can adjust to be more conservative if needed.

You will also need to consider the age pension in Australia. Once you reach aged pension age (currently 67), you can apply for the aged pension if your assets and income are under the thresholds. This substantially reduces the drawdown on assets in most cases and means that you can choose to target having enough money until 67, and then have the aged pension take over.

Everyone's needs are different when it comes to retirement, so it's best to use an online financial independence calculator to figure out what you need. These calculators often don't factor in two people, and may miss a variety of variables, so use these as a guide only. If you want a more specific and accurate number, you can reach out to a financial advisor, such as Guideway Wealth, for a financial health check.

How does living off your investments work?

Of course, it will take years, if not decades, to save the necessary amount to live solely off your investments. But don't forget that your money will compound over time.

As an example, if you invest $1000 a month for 30 years with a 7 per cent interest return, your money can grow to be $1.13 million (see figure 9.1). You would have only contributed $360 000 over the 30 years. Meanwhile, the interest earned on your investments would amount to $773 529. It's kind of like receiving more than $700 000 of free money just for investing regularly over the long term.

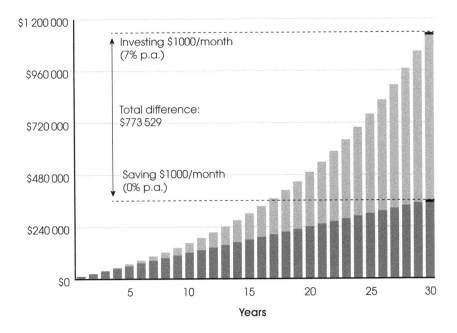

Figure 9.1: investing regularly over the long term pays off

Now, let's say you have $1 million invested and you are ready to retire. Your annual expenses are $40 000, which means you need $40 000 to live off. There are two things you can do:

1.   You can sell off $40 000 of your $1 million.

2.   You can live off the dividends from your invested $1 million.

3.   A mixture of both!

The first option is pretty self-explanatory. You sell down your shares and pay any applicable tax. If you're retired by this point (or have no/low income), this option may be preferable due to the high tax-free threshold in Australia. You'd currently need to sell approximately $56 000 worth of shares before triggering tax (assuming you have no other sources of taxable income).

The second one might need a little more explanation.

If you want to live off your dividends, you'll need to calculate your dividend yield (also referred to as equity yield). The calculation is simple: divide the annual dividend by the current share price to get the dividend yield:

Dividend yield percentage = Annual dividend per share / Share price × 100

So, if a company pays $5 in dividends per share and its share price is $200, the dividend yield would be 2.5 per cent.

You can find the dividend yield or payment in the ETF or the company's annual report, or by finding your payout through your share registry.

Going back to our example, where you have $1 million invested: let's say you have a 2.5 per cent dividend yield. You would be getting $25 000 per year, which won't be enough money if your expenses are $40 000 a year. However, if your dividend yield is 4 per cent, you'd be getting $40 000 a year in income.

It's worth noting that dividends are not fixed and can vary in amount. Some companies don't pay dividends at all. Therefore, dividend yield is a backward-looking indicator and not indicative of future dividends.

Furthermore, if your investments are in Australian companies, they may even have franking credits, which we discussed in the previous chapter, attached to them. Remember, dividends are also taxed at your marginal tax rate.

As we've seen, some ETFs are focused on higher dividend returns whereas others focus more on higher capital growth (the share price value).

Once you've accumulated enough money and assets to retire, most people will live off a mix of both 1 and 2: the income from their investments (dividends), and then sell a small portion of investments to fund the rest of their living costs. Over time, investments will decrease but that's okay. The goal here is to ensure that there's enough to support you over your lifetime.

It's valuable to understand what's best for your personal situation. Therefore, talking to a financial advisor or tax accountant about your investing and tax strategy may be advantageous.

Defining financial independence (FI)

For some investors, traditional retirement feels far away. You may want to retire early — or at least strive for FI — meaning you don't have to rely on traditional work to live.

Where FI differs from regular retirement is that instead of retiring in your 60s, the aim may be to achieve FI earlier, in your 40s or even your 30s. That way, if you want to quit your job or at least reduce your hours, you can. Or you can achieve FI at the regular retirement age and have the money to do whatever you want without being restricted by the aged pension.

It's a long-term journey that requires discipline, informed financial decisions and a long-term perspective. It also often requires a certain level of privilege since it's far easier to achieve for those on higher incomes or those who started investing at an early age. However, living frugally with the intent to invest and replace your salary with dividends is an admirable endeavour worth striving for regardless of your income level or age.

One of the ways to calculate when you will reach FI is by using the method described previously — that is, by investing 25 times your expenses. If you want to reach FI earlier in your life, you may need to account for different scenarios in the future. Someone who's retiring in their 60s has a shorter life timeframe than someone who wants to retire in their 40s. There's an additional 20 years that need to be considered.

For example, you may want to buy a bigger house or downsize in the future. You may want to fund your children's education. Or you may develop health issues that will cost a lot of money.

Considering various scenarios may be helpful in estimating whether 25 times your expenses is enough for you, or whether you need to save and invest more to reach FI.

Another way to calculate when you can reach FI is by understanding your savings rate, which determines how many years you have until you can reach FI.

American blogger Peter Adeney, who also goes by the name of Mr Money Moustache, states that you can determine your savings rate based on two things:

- your annual income

- your annual expenses.

For example, if you spend 100 per cent of your income, you will never be able to retire because you haven't saved and invested any money. However, if you spend 0 per cent of your income, you can retire right now because you have no expenses and don't need any money to live off. Those who strive for FI might calculate their savings rate (which really should be called an investment rate because it's the percentage you would theoretically invest), as shown in table 9.1, to work out how many years away they are from reaching FI.

Table 9.1: calculating your savings rate will help you determine when you can become financially independent

Savings rate (%)	Working years until FI
5	66
10	51
15	43
20	37
25	32
30	28
35	25
40	22
45	19
50	17
55	14.5
60	12.5
65	10.5
70	8.5
75	7
80	5.5
85	4
90	Under 3
95	Under 2
100	0

Source: Adapted from Mr Money Mustache, The Shockingly Simple Math Behind Early Retirement.

A higher savings rate means fewer years spent working towards FI. The lower the savings rate, the longer you have to work. If the goal is to not work forever, it may be a good idea to start tracking your savings rate to understand how much longer you need to work.

How does FI work with super?

If FI is a part of your investing strategy, you may need to consider how much you need to invest outside of your super to sustain your lifestyle until you can access your super. If you're planning on not working at all, you want to make sure you don't run out of money prior to traditional retirement. See figure 9.2.

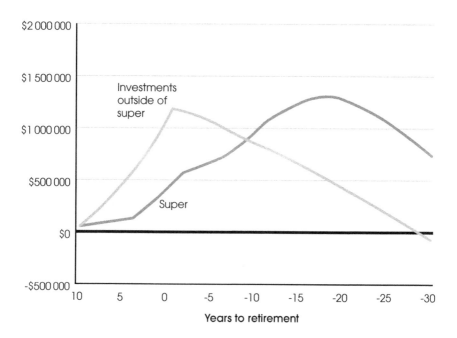

Figure 9.2: if super is part of your FI strategy, you may consider the optimal time to draw down your investments to fund your early retirement

As you move closer to FI, it's very likely your strategy, investments and risk tolerance will change and evolve. You may be less risk-averse and want more defensive assets to forgo market volatility.

Conversely, you may be more comfortable with extra growth assets in your super because you're not planning to access it in the short term.

A lot of planning and consideration goes into making a financial plan for FI and super, in which case it may be a good idea to talk to a professional financial planner.

For example, do you actually need 25 times your expenses saved up? Will you possibly get an inheritance that may change your financial situation? What about when your kids leave your house and you consider downsizing? Various scenarios are worth considering when planning for FI.

Different types of FI

Just as personal finance is personal, so is your journey to FI. In fact, that's why it's not a one-size-fits-all package. There are in fact a few different versions of FI. You may find that one of the following resonates with you.

- *Traditional FI.* This is the classic FI version we've mainly spoken about, where you're planning to have expenses that are similar to those you have right now and you've invested accordingly.

- *Lean FI.* Lean FI focuses more on a frugal lifestyle, where you are cutting costs to save and invest. This doesn't consider the luxuries in life, but rather just the necessities.

- *Fat FI.* This is at the other end of the spectrum and focuses on having a lavish lifestyle once you're financially independent. It allows for more spending and comfort.

- *Semi FI.* This option is a combination of the freedom that FI provides balanced with some paid work. If you feel like you've saved enough to reduce your hours at your paid gig, this may be an option for you. It's where you have the freedom and flexibility to work part-time since your investments are funding some of your income.

- *Coast FI.* If you feel as though you've saved enough in your super and don't need to add more to it, you may have reached Coast FI. You can still work, but you don't have to worry about funding your retirement.

- *Geo FI.* If you love to travel or want to live in a cheaper country where your money can go further, you may want to consider this option. There are some ethical considerations with Geo FI as it can have an impact on local economies.

Perhaps your FI journey doesn't fall into any of the categories above, and that's okay too. Only you know what's best for you.

How we think about FI

Ana: The idea of retiring early was very appealing to me when I was young and single. But my thoughts have changed over the years as my passive income has increased.

When I was on parental leave, I realised that even though I love spending time with my family, I still want to feel like I have a purpose. I focused on some personal projects and worked on the side occasionally. That provided me with some income, while still giving me the freedom to do things I love.

My version of FI probably falls under the semi FI category. I love work and I love freedom, so why not have both?

Tash: I came across the idea of FI very early on in my journey and initially loved the idea of retiring early. Like Ana, I probably resonate most with semi FI. I like having the freedom to travel, try new things and make money in a way that aligns with my values.

What's your idea of FI?

Investing enables you to have security, freedom and options. There's really no need for you to invest 25 times your expenses if that's not your goal. Sure, the idea of retiring early may sound appealing, but it doesn't mean it's for everyone.

Some of the principals around calculating your savings rate are helpful if you're thinking about keeping expenses low and investing the rest. But once you get a handle on these things and start automating your processes, you should be able to free up some time to focus on more important things — whatever those may be for you.

Because investing is a long journey, remember to celebrate wins along the way, such as your first investment, or the first time you reached $1000 or $10 000 or $100 000.

You can even celebrate by tracking the expenses your investments can cover — for example, one week of rent, or a 5-month holiday or even a 5-year sabbatical. Sometimes just focusing on the growth of your dividends can be exciting and motivating.

Whether you want to work forever or not, educating yourself through financial literacy is the first step in empowering your investing journey. With time and consistency, and the financial backing of an investment portfolio, you can build a life you love.

Make a start

How to live off your investments

- Calculate your annual expenses and multiply it by 25 to figure out what your 'FI number' is. This number is how much you would need invested to reach financial independence.

- Take a look at your investments and see if you can calculate the dividend yield and the capital growth.

- Figure out your savings rate by calculating what percentage you invest every month.

- Use a FI calculator to help you consider your investments both inside and outside of super.

- Take a moment to think about what your idea of financial independence is.

Case Study

Ro, 36

1. *Annual income*: $150k incl. super + potential bonus (max. 20%).

2. *Source of income*:

   Project Manager/YouTube content creator fulltime + starting side hustle (YouTube).

3. *What do you currently invest in?*

   Cash in offset: 46%; US stocks: 50%; AU Stocks/ETF: 4%.

4. *Investing platforms*: Stake and Pearler.

5. *What's the breakdown of your shares?*

   40% VAS, 30% VTS, 30% VEU.

6. *How much do you invest and how often?*

   $1k a month minimum.

7. *What are your money goals?*

   To safeguard my retirement and prepare my kids for success.

8. *How much debt do you have?*

   Mortgage: $1.1 million.

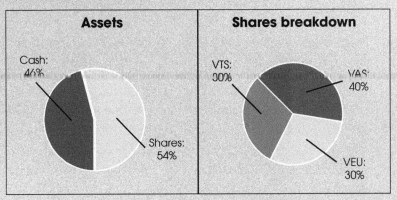

Assets	Shares breakdown
Cash: 46%	VTS: 30%
Shares: 54%	VAS: 40%
	VEU: 30%

9. *What's your biggest financial challenge?*

I love cars and tech so money is easily spent on them!

10. *What's your investing strategy?*

Based on world events, I have started to push some money into Aussie ETFs as opposed to individual stocks on Stake.

11. *What's your biggest money mistake?*

Spending it all in my teens/early 20s.

12. *Do you have any advice for new investors?*

The best way is to just do it. If you're scared, I would suggest micro-investing apps just so that you understand how things work and after that I would recommend looking further into investing. If you have the knowledge to understand how to micro-invest then you already know how to buy shares — whether it's ETFs or individual stocks.

13. *How are you building a life you love through investing?*

The short answer is that investing is the 'enabler' in our life to make certain things possible in the longer term (minimum 5 years). To break it down … if we continue to just have money sitting in our offset account or in a separate savings account, it's going to generate roughly a 5 per cent return based on our mortgage and that's really the 'limitation' of that. With investing and compounding, the sky's the limit. There will be great years and there will be bad ones — there's no doubt about that; however, through time, you should generally come out on top with a better result than just having that amount sitting in the bank.

The specifics around me saying that investing is the enabler will include things like private school for the kids (currently we are public and intend on staying public but the option is there if we are investing for the future), holidays, new cars and anything else we really want.

It'll put us in a position where we can (if we want) sell off some of these investments at a point in time in the future to fund whatever it is we want/need. If not, the money will just grow and will most likely just be passed onto our kids in the future.

Conclusion

Go on and live your best life

If you've read this far, you now have all the tools you need to make the best decisions for yourself so you can invest in your future, build a life you love and have options when it comes to *not* working forever.

In most cases, there's apprehension when we try something new: What if I get it wrong? What if I'm terrible at it? What if I'm not as successful as I hoped? But like all things, it takes time, practice and perseverance to reach your goals. Investing towards a life goal is exactly the same.

You won't become a perfect investor overnight and you won't be able to quit your job tomorrow. You might make mistakes along the way; you might even adjust your goals and portfolio every few years. And that's okay — that's normal. It's all a part of learning to become an investor.

Some of the best ways to learn a new skill is by actually doing it. No-one becomes an expert in a field overnight. It takes countless hours to home in on a skill, whether that be creating art, learning a sport or even investing. But that doesn't mean you need to wait until you have all the information before you do something.

Analysis paralysis is the killer of productivity. So, if you've come this far in the book and feel like you still don't have enough information to start investing and mapping out the life you love, we've got news for you: you're procrastinating. Let us give you the gentle push you need to start: you've got this!

If you need a recap, here are six steps to follow that will lead you towards a life where you don't have to work forever.

1. Write down your *why* and your investing and life goals

Investing is a long journey. Probably the longest journey towards a goal you'll ever have in your life — especially when you're considering your retirement. Therefore, you need to keep on track by ensuring you are motivated to stay the course.

Take note of why you're investing — and keep that in mind as you reach milestones along the way. Is it to leave your toxic job, security for your family or just to ensure you have enough to retire on? Whatever the reason, that is your guiding star. Hold onto that vision if you ever feel like you're wavering from your goal.

If anything is holding you back from starting, write it down and consider 'what's the worst thing that could happen?' Are you worried you'll make the wrong investment choice? Remember that you can always sell or adjust your strategy as needed. Are you scared you'll lose all your money? Remember that by diversifying and investing in low-cost index funds, you're reducing your risk and if for some reason the economy does crash, you won't realise any losses until you actually sell. Perhaps you don't think you'll have enough invested to quit your job or start your dream business. You can run the numbers and adjust them as needed to achieve your goals. Are you concerned you don't have enough information to get started? Don't let analysis paralysis get in the way. Again, you've got this.

Once you've written your 'worst case scenario' when it comes to investing and building a life you love, chances are it isn't as scary as you may have imagined.

Set some SMART goals for yourself. (Remember: SMART stands for specific, measurable, achievable, relevant and time-bound.) So, for example, a SMART goal may be to save $80 000 for a house deposit by saving $11 429 a year for 7 years. You can even break that goal down further by celebrating every month that you invest $953. Or perhaps your goal is to make $200 extra a month from your side hustle. That's about $47 a week. See? You've got this.

Remember to celebrate the wins along the way. Since investing and working towards your financial goals can be a long process, it's important to take note of what you accomplished — even if it's just automating your investments bimonthly. Chances are, you've picked up a new habit that will benefit you in the long run.

2. Make sure you're ready to invest

Investing can really change your life, but it's important to ensure you're financially secure and ready to take the leap. You need to have a safety net before you can start to build wealth.

Here's a checklist of all the things you should do before investing:

- Pay off any personal debt you may have.

- Save at least 3–6 months of expenses in an emergency fund.

- Budget for at least a month to have an understanding of your cash flow and how much you can invest.

- Allocate an amount (or percentage) of money every pay cheque that you can use to start investing.

- If you're struggling to find money to invest, consider reducing some of your expenses.

- Attempt to increase your income so you have more money to invest.

- Mentally prepare to invest — and remember, you've got this!

It's important to be prepared prior to investing. Since investing is for the long term, you want to future-proof yourself so you aren't tempted to dip into your investments. That's why it's advantageous to pay off consumer debt, have an emergency fund and have a strong grasp of your finances and budgeting.

Not having a handle on your finances can have a massive impact on your future wealth. Just imagine you don't have an emergency fund and something happens. You may be forced to sell shares at a time when the market has dipped, realising your losses and not allowing your investments to recover in value. Plus, there are tax consequences, and you'd miss out on the compounding effect of your investments.

Having good financial health also comes down to really understanding and tracking your budget so you can find more money to invest with. By reducing your expenses and increasing your income you can grow the gap and make it easier to invest.

Plus, if you live on less money, you will need less money for your future self because your expenses are already low! There's a compounding effect to your actions as well — how cool!

3. Have a positive money mindset

For those of you who've reached this part of the book and haven't invested yet, take a moment to consider if there's anything holding you back. If there is, what is it? Write it down and try to see if you can adjust your mindset around it to overcome any barriers you may have to investing.

If the underlying thought is *I'm just not ready yet*, we've got three words for you:

You are ready!

You've just read a whole book on investing. Chances are you've been thinking about it for a while. The only thing getting in the way of you building your wealth right now is you.

You've got this. You just need to start.

4. Decide what to invest in

Investing can sound complicated: what to invest in, how much and for how long? The reality is you can always adjust your strategy.

Like most things in life, it isn't set in stone. If you realise in a year's time that you'd rather invest in more ethical funds, you can change your investments. If you think you'd like a more conservative portfolio of bonds, you can add them in. Or if you want to add a thematic fund — one that focuses on a specific theme that aligns with your values — you can do that too!

The point is, you can always adjust as you go.

However, if you're just starting out, it may be wise to start with one low-cost index fund. This way you get an idea of how to invest, what to look for, how dividends work and whether it suits your needs.

To help you decide what to invest in you could:

- look at your superannuation and see what it's invested in to give you an idea of what funds are made up of

- look at some of the most commonly invested-in ETFs online (Pearler ranks its top invested-in ETFs on its website)

- find a risk-tolerance test online so you have an idea of how much risk you're willing to take with your investments

- consider what assets you're planning to invest in and what percentage you will allocate to each

- consider how your goals align with your long-term investment strategy.

Remember that you can invest in various asset classes: cash, bonds, shares and property. As you build wealth, you can always adjust the percentages of assets you hold. This also changes throughout your life as you buy property or shares, or even sell down assets in retirement. Knowing you have flexibility can empower you to just get started and learn.

5. Sign up to a brokerage account

Investing in shares is as easy as buying shoes online. Just as you have to sign up to Amazon, for example, you have to sign up to a broker to purchase ETFs. Online brokers are similar to online marketplaces such as Amazon, and will facilitate your purchase. Most brokers charge a fee when you buy and sell (think of it like the credit card fee that merchants use).

Since brokers deal with money and securities, you will need to verify your identity with your ID and take the time to fill out the proper documentation — but after that it's easy!

Some beginner investors get hung up about choosing the right broker and lament about finding the one with the lowest fees or best features. But as we've seen, it's less important *where* you buy and more important *what* you buy.

Some things to consider when you're looking for a broker that aligns with your goals:

- Does the broker facilitate CHESS, custodian or micro-investing?

- What are the fees per transaction?

- Is it easy to use?

- Does it have all the features you need?

- Are you able to automate your investing?

If you're not sure which broker is best suited to you, you can always sign up to a few different ones, try them all out and see which one works best.

In many cases, especially if you hold CHESS-Sponsored shares, you can also transfer to a different broker as easily as switching bank accounts.

6. Buy ETFs

Okay, you've decided what to invest in, you've opened a brokerage account, and now you're ready to pull the pin and become an investor. How exciting!

There are various ETFs that might align with your strategy. Some may be global ETFs that hold international companies from around the world from various industries. Or you may choose specific ones that hold only Australian companies.

Whatever you choose, make sure to check that it's low cost and diversified. Remember, you can always adjust your portfolio if you need or want to.

When buying your first ETF, you will need to register with a share registry, which manages and records who the shareholders of a share or ETF are. When you register with a share registry, you can also decide what to do with your dividends: have them paid out to you or reinvest them.

This is an extremely exciting time because it's the beginning of your investing journey!

Congrats! You're an investor!

How exciting: you've now officially gone through the process of empowering yourself to build wealth for the future. Not only is that remarkable, but you are now a shareholder — an official investor. Good on you!

Now go on and live a life you love!

***

Continue learning with us. Subscribe to the *Get Rich Slow Club* podcast wherever you get your podcasts.

Join our Facebook group by searching the 'Get Rich Slow Club'.

Follow us on socials! @tashinvests, @anakresina, @getrichslowclub